FREE 2 EARN 4 EVER

By
S.J. August

Library of Congress Cataloging-in-Publication Data

August, S.J., 2012-.

Free 2 Earn 4 Ever by S.J. August presents a straightforward solution to the current economic crisis that will give everyone an equal chance to earn money / S. J. August.

p.   cm.
ISBN-10: 0615586066
ISBN-13: 978-0615586069
LCCN: 2012932420

Cover Illustration by Richard Hagen.
Interior illustrations by Richard Hagen.
Interior layout and cover layout by CreateSpace.

This book is available at special quantity discounts to use as premiums and special promotions, or for use in training or classroom settings. For more information, please email your request to Free2Earn2012@gmail.com or visit the website www. Free2Earn4Ever.com.

This book was made possible by the talented editing, copy writers, and layout and design resources at CreateSpace.

CONTENTS

INTRODUCTION

Psalm 69:33

This book will take you on a journey into the future of how people will earn livings, supplement their incomes, and change their lives. I am an idea person, a visionary, not in the sense of fortune-telling or psychic powers, but in terms of envisioning what we as a generation can create. I grew up inventing things, fascinated by *Popular Science,* and obsessed with entrepreneurship.

I worked in a corporate job for over a decade, and the way people complained about work while dreaming of retirement baffled me. How can people ignore their mind and body's plea to change the way they are living? We were not meant to do the same thing for forty or more hours every week. Health problems, mental problems, and loss of zest for life take their toll after years of shoving down the inner desire to pursue hobbies and interests. Antidepressant usage is at an all-time high, and I believe the continual suppression of actual living is somehow related.

The standard of living has increased in the United States and in other parts of the world, but at what cost? Statistics indicate that most people are unhappy with their current jobs. Many dream of early retirement and doing something different, but they don't do it because of a myriad of reasons. The biggest one is money.

In my own search for a way to financial freedom, I started an online business. Using my business and marketing degrees, I was able in four short years to surpass the amount of money

I had earned in the corporate environment. I know what extra cash can do for a person; with my extra money, I was able to buy my first home, take vacations, buy a newer car, and buy things I wanted.

When I worked in the corporate environment, I heard many others talk about their dreams of breaking out of the workplace, staying home with their kids, working from home somehow, and starting a business. One coworker in particular had just had her first baby, and it was difficult for her to leave her twelve-week-old at a daycare facility all day while she sat at a desk and did mundane work, but she had bills to pay. I wanted to use my idea mind to help her, so I would come in every day with suggestions for businesses she could start that would give her the ability to work from home. It is difficult to leave a steady paycheck and take that leap of faith into a new way of earning money, but trying to bring in money with the little time you have left after a long day at the office is draining, especially with children and a family to tend to.

One weekend in September 2010, my daughter and I were driving from Minneapolis to Duluth. About thirty minutes into the two-hour trip, I was telling her all my business ideas. My idea mind was in complete overdrive, frantically searching for the winning plan. Some of my ideas were really good, and others were only average. I was jumping from one idea to the next in a blizzard of possibilities, not letting my daughter get a word in at all. Suddenly I stopped and said a prayer. "Please, God, help me to clear my mind and choose the business I'm supposed to focus on." In an instant, at mile marker 169 northbound 35W, my mind cleared, and I had a clear vision of the idea I'm going to explain in this book. I saw into the future. I saw people's faces. I saw how the roads looked different. The cars were different, and the people were different. It is very difficult to describe. The biggest change I saw was that people were smiling, they had hope in their eyes, and their passion was back. They were excited and full of purpose. They were spending time with their families and friends. They owned their time. They were no longer prisoners of worry and stress.

This wasn't a psychic vision. It was the kind of vision an inventor sees when he imagines people using his invention. Inventors see things that others cannot. They see their products, and, more importantly, they see their products' impact on the world.

My favorite scenes in the *Back to the Future* movie are of Doc Brown in his garage laboratory. He would get so excited when his ideas allowed him to see the future. He saw opportunity and change. He knew his ideas would change the world.

This type of vision is what I was blessed with. The idea I was given in that moment of clarity will change the world. In this book I will explain the necessary technologies that are already being used, but they are not being used together for maximum benefit for the masses. Like puzzle pieces laid out on a table, they just need to be rearranged and fitted together to create a picture of living that is like nothing this world has ever seen. Never before has the world had the ability to share ideas, knowledge, and entertainment like this. More importantly, those that participate in this will be compensated for their efforts. Compensation is the most crucial piece of the puzzle.

I believe that our economies are hurting because there is such a mercy factor involved in earning a living. Restrictions are placed on us today like the bondage that people in Moses time felt. We may not even realize these shackles, because we've lived with them all along. It's just the way it is; we don't know any different.

It is my hope that this book will help you understand the Free 2 Earn 4 Ever idea and get you excited about how it could better your life, your family's lives, your friends' lives, and the lives of people around the world. I hope you tell everyone you know about this. Rally for it. Don't allow companies to say it can't be done. If they say they cannot do it, or if they bring up all the reasons why it won't work, don't stand for it.

For those of you who say it won't work or can think of a boat-load of reasons why it shouldn't happen, I suggest that you solve the problems. Use your smarts to overcome the issues and road-blocks. You have an opportunity to be part of a generation that created a video revolution. Just like other revolutions in history, this is a pivotal shift for mankind.

ACKNOWLEDGEMENTS

I would like to thank the following people for their assistance, feedback, and insight:

Hailey, Amy, Jeremy, and Richard.

CHAPTER 1

"I predict future happiness for Americans if they can prevent the government from wasting the labors of the people under the pretense of taking care of them."

-Thomas Jefferson

Our Current Economic Situation

Why focusing on jobs is the wrong answer.

In America right now, there is a continuous outcry for jobs. News sources continually report on stories with the phrases, "We need more jobs," "We have to cut taxes to help big corporations create more jobs," and "Jobs will revive our sick economic situation."

Jobs are not the only answer to fixing our economy. If you do some "why drilling" (asking yourself "why" questions), you'll find the root of the problem. I've found that the root problem is that a large and growing number of people are not participating in the core activities that fuel a strong economy—earning and spending. As more people spend less, others earn less, and as people earn less, they spend less. Slowly a healthy economy breaks down.

Here is a quick "why drilling" example:

We need jobs.

Why?

People will be back at work earning money.

Why is that important?

They will be able to pay their bills and buy things.

Why is that important?

When they pay their bills or buy things, it gets money moving so that *others* can earn money to pay their bills and buy things.

The solution for an unhealthy economy is to get money moving again by increasing the number of people earning and spending.

One of the reasons money has been so unevenly distributed in this country is that, for most people, sources of money are few and are mostly fixed or closely linked to time. For example, if you are an employee, you are paid for your time. You punch a clock to get paid for hours worked or receive a salary that is limited by an employer's perceived value of your time commitment. Once a person has a full-time job, or sometimes two or three jobs, he or she is at maximum capacity of exchanging time for a paycheck. More jobs will not help this person. Any time you are in a position where your earnings are fixed to a certain amount of time, you are pretty well locked into that earning level, unless you look for other sources of income or revenue streams.

If you take a look at successful corporations or wealthy people and their revenue "earn" streams, you will find that they do not depend on their "earn" to come from one source but rather build and rely upon multiple sources of revenue. A successful business diversifies and finds multiple ways to bring in money. For example, a corporation grows its product lines or markets to different customer segments rather than providing only one product to one customer group. Likewise, a wealthy person normally has multiple ways of bringing in money, such as multiple businesses and a variety of investments. There is security in knowing that money is coming in from multiple sources for the simple reason that if the revenue stops or slows from one source, revenue is still received from one or multiple other sources.

Many people today rely on only one source for their "earn." This singular reliance can cause stress and financial uncertainty. Discovering that your one "earn" source will stop providing to you would cause great worry and concern. When your only source does stop and your "earn" is gone, what then? You would have to scramble to find another way to earn money. This is a real situation for the millions of unemployed people today.

Below are some common ways people earn money. Many have used number six to supplement one or more of the other methods.

Ways people (not companies) earn money:

1. Be an employee.

   This means a person works for someone else, looking to another person or company as a source of money or "earn."

2. Own a business.

   People sell services or products as a source of their "earn."

3. Receive government funds (Social Security, disability, welfare).

   Many people contend that this is not really earning money, so we will just note that this method is getting money. I believe that many who depend on this source of "earn" would rather not but have found themselves in situations where, for various reasons, they cannot get money from any of the other sources.

4. Receive core earnings from interest on savings or pension payouts. The majority of people with this source of income are retired people earning interest on money saved during their earlier years or pensions built up from working many years as an employee.

5. Receive royalties or earnings on previously sold goods or services.

    This group includes business owners, inventors, and others who have sold services, such as actors or musicians.

6. Sell stuff.

    A source of "earn" for many people today is selling their stuff. Personal sales on Internet sites such as eBay, Etsy, and Craigslist have recently seen incredible growth. You could also generate "earn" by selling things at a garage sale, to a pawn shop, or in classified ads.

The Government's role

The stimulus money that President Obama put into the economy in 2010 in an effort to jumpstart the economy[1] was temporary and too small, but it was on the right track, following the idea that people need money to spend money. When people spend money at an increasing rate, others earn money at an increasing rate, whether it be companies or individuals. I believe the purpose of the stimulus money was to provide money to people so they spend it and help create demand for jobs. However, I have two problems with this stimulus plan:

1. A flat-rate payout does not impact everyone the same. The amount received will be more valuable to someone earning $20,000 a year than to a higher wage earner.

2. How much of the stimulus money actually stayed active in the U.S. economy, being passed from one U.S. spender to another? My hunch is that large retailers saw an increase in sales that created a higher demand for foreign-made products.

---

1. Brian Wingfield and Joshua Zumbrun, "Stimulus? Yes, In 2010," Forbes.com, January 28, 2009, accessed February 8, 2012, http://www.forbes.com/2009/01/28/economy-stimulus-unemployment-congress-business-washington_0128_stimulus.html.

So who benefited from these small stimulus payouts—large corporations and foreign business owners (made in China)? Where do you think the money ended up?

There have been suggestions made recently that the U.S. government should give corporations tax credits so they can hire more employees. However, businesses hire employees when there is an actual demand for more employees. Hiring is driven by an increasing demand for businesses to output more products and services. If a corporation were to hire people just because the government will give them money for doing so, the resulting decrease in unemployment would create a false impression of a rebounding economy.

It is not only the amount of money in the economy that is important, but also the constant movement of money among the majority of the population. You can have a lot of currency in an economy, but if everyone hangs on to it and doesn't spend it in a way that allows other people in the same economy to earn and spend, it doesn't help.

Think of the board game Monopoly. The game can go on for a very long time if the players continue to interact with each other in buying and selling properties. If a player runs out of or gets low on money, the other players also cannot buy and sell properties because they depend on the interaction from the other players. Players who run out of money are out of the game.

People also need money in the real world to keep "playing" in our economy. Some have much more money than others, and some have very little. If players continually exchange money between each other without going to the banker for it, the banker (the government) will not run out of money, and the game continues. If the banker continually taxes the players in every exchange, it creates a banker's game in which the banker holds the majority of the money and can spend wisely or unwisely to keep players exchanging. This can also put the players in the position of depending on and being at the mercy of the banker. If the banker puts a lot of the money into another game (another country), fewer players can stay actively involved because the money is on another game board (in a foreign economy). The less money the players have, the more cautious they are to exchange it.

Step out of the game mentality for a moment and think about where our economy's money is being spent. When someone buys an item, where does that money go? Is it put back into the economy and spent again to keep people interacting and exchanging, or does the majority of that money go to people who store the money in their own pockets? How much of our money ends up on a large corporation's balance sheet or in an executive's bonus check? How much of our money goes to foreign countries? This may not be a bad thing, because if we as a nation learn from it more about the impact of our spending choices, it was all worth lesson learned.

The money that is in our economy needs to be shuffled around to get more people involved in the exchange so they can participate and be prosperous. The more people participate, the more we experience prosperity because we can then buy what we need and want.

So how can we get money moving or exchanging here in the U.S.? We need to make sure there is ample opportunity to succeed in this needed exchange of money, and not just for the affluent or well-educated members of our society. A country is made up of all of its people, not just the elite few. Our society consists of people from many different generations, education levels, physical abilities, and cultural backgrounds.

Government and the Private Sector

A government's role in the economy is to not attack the invisible hand that guides growth and expansion. Our government has been guilty of this by bailing out failing or corrupt industries, paying companies to hire employees, and making itself responsible for creating jobs in the private sector. The government's role is to focus on creating an environment where its citizens can thrive and prosper.

Over the last decade, there has been a shift in who Americans look to for economic revival. In early days of this country, it was the private sector that led growth into the Industrial Revolution, with the government playing a supporting role. As we forge forward into the Information Age, we now tend to look to the government instead of the private sector as the leader to provide for the citizens.

Jobs

Let's look at jobs as we know them today, leaving out the self-employed for now. With the constant outcry for jobs, let's examine what we are really asking for. If you have a job, you are considered employed, and you do something for someone else's gain. There are millions of different types of jobs. You can go do factory line work, and you can sit at a desk forty hours a week, but at what cost? What are you exchanging for that paycheck? The answer is your time and your skills.

Those who do have jobs today are so busy getting up and going to work that they come home only to have just a few hours to themselves. Many stuck in that consistent grind are just barely able to afford the basic necessities of life. Some take on additional jobs to make ends meet. They see their children only occasionally, and when they do see them, they are so worn out from working and worried about providing for them that their moods are sour.

What about those who already have a job (maybe a couple jobs) and still cannot afford to take care of their families? Will more jobs help them? Do they want a third or fourth job?

In addition, as baby boomers get too old to work at a job, how can they continue to earn money? Some baby boomers leave the workforce early due to medical reasons or death of a spouse. On the other end of the spectrum, there are some baby boomers who realize that the utopian retirement they worked and saved for all their life was a mirage and will not be realized in their lifetime because rising medical and living costs force them to continue to work.

Don't get me wrong; there are some extremely positive things about jobs. Jobs are not all bad, but statistically, the majority of employees in America are only "somewhat satisfied" with their current position and are actively looking for other employment.[2] In addition, people are going to college for degrees in lines of work in which they never get a job. Why? What happens between the time people sign up to dedicate four years of their life to study a certain subject and the time they receive their diploma and look for a job? Many find that their dreams of working in that particular field fade over the course of those four years.[3]

I recently talked with a coworker who told me he originally went to school to become a meteorologist. He said that when he was younger he was fascinated with weather, but he realized after graduation that the salary range in that field was not what he wanted to be stuck with, and the jobs that would earn the level of money he wanted were few and difficult to get. In order to earn more money, he had to change careers.

I don't believe jobs are the solution to our economy's problems. They are part of the solution, but not the answer. The real thing we need to get the economy healthy again is to increase the number of people involved in the exchange of money through "earn and spend" activities. The more people are involved in earning and spending, the healthier the economy will be.

---

2. *Escape from Corporate America*, "The Latest Job Satisfaction Stats," February 5, 2009, http://www.escapefromcorporate.com/the-latest-job-satisfaction-stats/

3. Richard Vedder, "Why Did 17 Million Students Go To College?," *Innovations* (blog), *The Chronicle of Higher Education*, October 20, 2010, http://chronicle.com/blogs/innovations/why-did-17-million-students-go-to-college/27634.

The Free 2 Earn 4 Ever initiative will provide an opportunity for more people to participate in economic activities than ever experienced in the history of humankind. It will be an enormous paradigm shift for the world.

▶

CHAPTER 2

"We can't solve problems by using the same kind of thinking we used when we created them."

-Albert Einstein

Free 2 Earn 4 Ever

*A*nyone should have the ability to upload a video about anything, put a price on it, and sell it to anyone willing to pay to watch it. In other words, online videos should be treated as products, which will make the world a better place. This simple change—thinking of online videos as products—could revolutionize how people earn their money. You may be skeptical, but if you see the benefits of this shift, the opportunities for prosperity will become apparent.

The New Roles Needed

Host Company

A host company will host the videos, and that is all. The host company will not act as a video approver, choosing which ones can be sold and which ones cannot; instead, video uploaders will determine the value of their videos and will price them accordingly. The host company will only provide the website and global tools that allow uploaders, viewers, and theme assemblers to do business with each other. The website will also provide tools to encourage usage—search functions, ratings, running time reports, video editing tools, etc. (see my later chapter on features and benefits for a full list).

Video Uploader

People or companies will be needed to upload videos to host companies' websites. Uploaders will maintain ownership of the video and will determine whether the video is free or if there should be a fee to watch it. If the uploader places a fee on the video, the uploader will also decide the price. If a video is determined illegal for copyright or other reasons, the uploader is legally responsible for the video, not the host company. This is a big change, since video hosting sites today hold the position that they are somewhat responsible for the videos they host. This mentality is impeding the progression of videos being treated as products.

Viewer

People will be needed to watch videos. Viewers can choose to watch free videos or videos they must pay to watch. I will go into more detail in my Feature and Benefits chapter for all the things viewers can do, such as watch previews and give ratings.

Theme Assembler

People or companies will be needed to find similar videos from one or many uploaders and to present the videos to viewers with a marked-up price. The marked-up price compensates the theme assemblers for their efforts. These people really act like retailers do in the offline environment; they offer convenience to viewers by assembling videos that appeal to a certain audience segment. There would be no need for video uploaders and theme assemblers to ever communicate or coordinate.

A New Type of Video Host Company

We need video hosting companies that treat online videos as products owned by video uploaders and allow uploaders to choose whether or not to charge people a fee. We need host companies that give anyone the freedom to earn.

The ideal video host company would allow any legal video to be posted and the price to be determined by the uploader. This would be similar to how a website hosting company works. Web hosting companies like GoDaddy.com let websites owned by another person or company live on their servers. Most hosting companies do not make site owners prove that their sites will be popular or that they will not contain controversial subjects.

Similarly, eBay allows people and companies to sell their products through eBay's website. Websites like eBay don't dictate the price or allow only popular items to be posted. If that was true, we may have never had the sale of Jesus toast. Everyone should be free to sell whatever they want for whatever price they want to charge. Ultimately it is the buyer who decides whether or not to make the purchase.

Easy to Buy

To increase sales, as any good marketer will tell you, you have to make it easy for customers to make the purchase. There are two main components in the Free 2 Earn 4 Ever program that will make it easy for viewers to buy online videos.

Money exchange

Just as you can go to iTunes and buy an app or music that someone else created, you should be able to buy a video that someone else created. The iTunes store sells apps and music from not just the big record companies and tech companies, but also individuals, too. Bloomberg Businessweek featured an article about a sixteen-year-old who created an app and had already earned $33,000 from it.[4]

Prepaid online video cards should be available to purchase in retail stores, just like iTunes cards. These cards allow customers who would not use a credit card online to still purchase from online stores. Some examples of customers who would not use credit cards online are children, those who don't own credit cards, and those who have security concerns about entering their credit card numbers online. You can bet that fewer purchases would be made on iTunes if kids had to ask their parents for the credit card every time they wanted to buy music. Prepaid cards make it easy for customers to buy.

Find what you're looking for

Videos should be purchasable and viewable when embedded on other websites. For example, a person blogging about cats should be able to embed a video on his or her blog site, not just provide a link over to the video hosting company. This technology of embedding videos is already in use, and many websites embed videos within their own web pages, even though those videos are actually hosted on sites like Vimeo or YouTube. This functionality needs to continue to help potential paying viewers find videos they want to buy.

The ability to find videos of a certain subject and present them in a way that is easy for consumers to find them will result in higher viewer satisfaction, which in turn will result in higher sales. No viewer wants to search through pages of irrelevant videos to find videos that interest them. A video uploader may possibly have videos on a myriad of subjects, forcing viewers to search through videos in which they have no interest.

---

4. George Anders, "Computer Camp: No Canoes, Just Coding (and Kickball)," *Bloomberg Businessweek*, August 4, 2011, http://www.businessweek.com/magazine/computer-camp-no-canoes-just-coding-and-kickball-08042011.html.

There is a correlation between visual and material products. Both material products and video products are created by a manufacturer or content owner. Sometimes a manufacturer creates products all related to each other, which means that all that manufacturer's products are all targeted to one customer group. However, a large number of manufacturers create products designed for a wide variety of customer segments. For example, a metal manufacturer may make parts for both sewing machines and chainsaws. Companies that manufacture products for different types of customers often obtain the help of distributors or retailers to get their products in front of the customers most likely to want to buy them. Rarely do customers purchase directly from the manufacturer.

Sometimes the same part is sold for different purposes, as well. For example, a sheet of metal may be sold to an airplane manufacturer, an arts and craft store, or a homebuilder. The same is true for video uploaders. Their videos could appeal to a wide variety of customer segments. For example, a little old grandma may have videos about when she worked as a nurse in a war, presenting parenting tips from raising six children, or showing off her gun collection. People looking for parenting tips may not be interested in seeing grandma's gun collection videos or listening to her war stories.

This is the problem with today's video websites. The videos are just out there, and they are not organized very well at all. If you find a really great video like MrArturoTrejo's video "Interview with a One-Year-Old,"[5] it is difficult to find more videos by other uploaders that are of the same humor type.

The retailer's role in the online video industry is played by what I refer to as theme assemblers. These folks are very important, because they help organize and segment videos to make it

5. "Interview with a One-Year-Old," YouTube video, 3:46, posted by MrArturoTrejo, May 19, 2011, http://www.youtube.com/user/MrArturoTrejo#p/u/0/bq2T7jP7dpQ.

easier for viewers to find what they want, thus increasing sales of videos overall.

Just a like a retailer marks up a price to compensate for assembling similar products for buyers' convenience, a theme assembler too should have the ability to mark up a price on a video. Viewers purchasing a video should only see the retail price. When you walk into a brick and mortar store, you don't see the prices the retailer paid for the items for sale; you see the prices at which the retailer is selling the items. For example, if you are a theme assembler and one of the video collections you market to customers is all antique guns, you may pick up grandma's video about her gun collection. She may have a price of fifty cents on it, and you mark it up to a dollar. As a theme assembler, you would have a store of videos you have determined as qualified to be presented together. If a viewer previews the video and agrees to pay a dollar to watch grandma's video, grandma earns fifty cents, and you earn fifty cents, minus the small percentage kept by the host company for making the transaction possible.

This entire idea boils down to the core belief that people should have the option to be compensated for their efforts. No one should be forced to work for free. Technology should provide the tools to earn revenues from providing a product (online video) or service (assembling similar videos for the convenience of the viewer).

There are some people who take other people's original videos and present them as their own. This is known as pirating videos, and is done for the opportunity to earn money from something people want to see. The theme assembler role will give people the opportunity to earn money without pirating.

Current opportunities to earn video money

Some people are already earning money from videos they have uploaded, but not in the capacity they could be. Many online video websites like YouTube give popular videos the opportunity to share in advertising revenue. Video uploaders agree to abide by the host company's guidelines and allow advertisements to play before their videos start or to appear as a banner across the bottom of their videos. Other video hosting sites may show ads on videos at their own discretion without offering uploaders the opportunity to share in the revenue from that advertising.

In either case, viewers are forced to first watch a commercial or advertisement before they can view the videos they wanted to see. Then, when the video does appear, banner advertisements continually appear at the bottom of the screen over the top of the video. Some viewers find this to be extremely annoying.

When viewers click on one of the banner advertisements at the bottom of the screen, it will pop open another window that takes them to the advertiser's website. The uploader gets money every time a viewer clicks on the banner ads, and they can also receive money when an advertisement plays at the beginning of their video. This is only for popular uploaders and those that meet certain content requirements. YouTube's Partner guidelines state:

> We are currently focusing on accepting users who regularly produce videos intended for a wide audience or who publish popular or commercially successful videos in other ways (such as DVDs sold online). In evaluating applications, we look at various factors including but not limited to the popularity of the user's videos, number of subscribers, the user's involvement with the YouTube community, and the user's track record of compliance with the YouTube terms of service.[6]

It is understandable that each individual company wants to set its own rules and guidelines, and a video hosting company can

6. YouTube's Partnerships Qualifications & FAQ, accessed February 9, 2012, http://www.youtube.com/t/partnerships_faq.

choose the videos they host and their own rules regarding compensation. Each business has the right to determine what it will and will not do.

▶

CHAPTER 3

"Man keeps inventing things all the time."

-Mikhail Kalashnikov

What the World Could Be

This chapter is written as if online video marketing was already available and in place. Imagine with me that anyone anywhere can already upload videos and charge people to view them. Journey with me into the future and see the freedoms we have been missing out on.

Retirement

People are no longer living in anticipation of a utopian phase of their life. They have learned that many have not survived to reach retirement in their later years, and those who have survived have found that their bodies are no longer able to carry out the dreams their younger selves strived for. Delaying retirement activities until a person's last years of life is now considered foolish. Many people now realize that the term "retirement" was created by the financial industry as a way to use other people's money in the form of "investments." Retirement made sense when people earned money during only one phase of their life and then no longer had a way to earn new money. Now that people can earn at any age, up to and beyond their death, "retirement" is dead.

Spending the prime of your life stuck in a job that leaves you with no free time and no time to raise your children, care for those you love, or simply enjoy life is a terrible waste. This delay has cost society financially through Social Security, welfare, and Medicare expenses, but even more costly, delaying life for some future time has ruined families, relationships, mental health, and population dynamics. Since we are now more in control of our ability to earn money, we enjoy career changes, spending time with family and friends, hobbies, travel, relocation, and relaxation as part of our everyday lives. We have freedom because we are no longer shackled to our paychecks.

College

For many years, many people hid behind the excuse that they didn't have enough money to go to college. This excuse is no longer tolerated. There is a surge of people returning to college, not only to earn degrees, but to take random classes that relate to their interests or passions.

Since the skill is so highly desired, almost all colleges now offer courses teaching how to create videos. Many college students are creating videos that show their life at school, as well as their challenges, daily routines, and parties. These videos are being watched by people shopping for colleges to attend, who watch the videos to see for themselves whether students enjoy the school and to gain a better understanding of what life is like at that particular college. These videos provide more information than could ever be presented in a college brochure or campus tour.

Many students posting college life videos earn enough revenue from their videos that they no longer need to take on jobs for spending cash, but can instead focus on their studies. In addition, the revenue they earn from these videos helps pay for their college tuition and will continue to bring them revenue for possibly the rest of their life and beyond.

Building Legacies

Once a video is uploaded, it can continue to earn money for decades, possibly even beyond the uploader's lifetime. Many uploaders choose to move their revenue into a trust for their future generations. Never before have so many people had the opportunity to provide for posterity. Baby boomers who were once worried whether they had enough savings for retirement are now wondering what do to with their revenue streams long term. Many are working with lawyers to ensure their grandchildren and favorite charities are the recipients of their earnings after they are gone.

The videos shot today will still be purchased a hundred years from now. Having the ability to hear the voices of the past and see how people lived has always been a fascination of humankind. Now, like never before, there is an opportunity to see how generations lived before us. People of the future will be able to see what was important to this generation, the tools they used, and their relationships with each other. It is like watching a replay in football and analyzing what went right and what went wrong. We are capturing life today on video for posterity's gain.

Innovation

With more people able to fund their own business start-ups using online video revenue, the number of patents and new products has exploded. Time and money are two crucial ingredients needed for innovation. Instead of being consumed with just earning a living from their jobs, sometimes working and commuting forty to sixty hours per week, people now have time to tinker and explore their ideas.

Viewers can now financially support innovation in areas they most care about. Many viewers are watching great inventors and scientists create the products, medical breakthroughs, and ideas that will revolutionize the future. Scientists invite the camera into their labs, explain their theories, and demonstrate how they plan to cure diseases, create new forms of energy, and many other wonderful breakthroughs.

Viewers are able to watch inventors' videos of trial and error that led them to final and patented products. The revenue earned from the videos gives these inventors the money they need to move their products from idea to market. In the past, great inventions would often sit in the patented phase, never to become reality, because of lack of funding. Now great inventions achieve consumer buy-in early in the process and are more successful because viewers feel so connected to the new products. No longer do inventors have to wait for a few investors to approve their endeavors. Instead, it is the people who nominate, through their paid viewership, the products of the future.

Children

Never before have there been so many children under the age of eighteen who are classified as the top earners in their families. Teens and tweens have stepped up to help their families understand the earning potential in online video sales. Many record video interviews of their grandparents and parents talking about their life experiences.

Many children have saved their entire college tuition before they enter high school. Their video earnings allow their family to spend more time together exploring hobbies, traveling, and working in charity.

Children previously were considered "on the bench" until they finished their schooling. After graduating from college, they were free to join life by working or pursuing what they wanted. However, the value of a child's fresh mind and perspective is now being harnessed and used to the family's advantage. No longer do mothers have to work two and three jobs to support their children, only to have them raised by a daycare or run the streets. Now families can work together to earn money and create the lives they want.

Kids are filming their perspectives on life, hobbies (like skateboarding, biking, swimming, and sporting competitions), and entertainment. Some of the sitcoms kids are creating attract millions of regular viewers, a higher viewership than many of the previous television shows.

Kids now have the same earning potential as adults, which is changing the products that are made and marketed to this group. Businesses have created a wide variety of new products and services specifically for this age group. The auto industry has seen the biggest change. Now that so many sixteen-year olds have the cash to buy vehicles when they first get their driver's licenses, auto manufacturers are exploring more high-tech cars loaded with custom features. Surprisingly, it is not the cost of fuel that drives this change, but the inventive, unrestrained minds of the young. The purchase of vehicles at a price of $100,000 is not uncommon.

Education

Alternative schools and learning plans, such as unschooling, have skyrocketed to allow children and their families more freedom with their time. It has long been known that the best learning doesn't take place in a classroom setting. Instead, children are now able to visit places of historic relevance or participate in other hands-on learning activities. They are now able to watch videos to learn more on a certain subject. They are also able to view multiple sides of issues as spoken by the advocates themselves. This is producing more well-rounded and educated children able to form their own opinions and thoughts.

Children's passion for learning is at its highest. They now feel more in control of their lives and want to pursue their interests. Previously, their interests may not have fit into a traditional job or may have confined them to low-paying positions, which often caused adults to discourage children from pursuing that subject.

Post-secondary education has changed, as well. No longer are people taking college courses to get into a job, but are instead pursuing subjects that interest them and gaining knowledge that will fuel their passions.

Traditional jobs

Previously, many jobs were held by people solely for the earning potential and prestige those positions offered, not because they were what people dreamed passionately of doing. People in these jobs could easily be spotted by the lack of interest they showed in their jobs. They worked for the paycheck and the weekend. This resulted in stagnant businesses and slowed innovation.

With the ability to earn money from online videos, people now have the freedom to take a lower-paying position because they are already able to earn the level of money their standard of living requires. Many lower-paying positions now have an abundance of applicants because people are actually very interested in their jobs. People may have been interested in doing a particular job before, but it meant their earnings would be extremely low, and they chose not to pursue it. For example, someone who loves being a tour guide but earns very little can now work in that position and still have unlimited earning potential through their online videos.

There has also been a shift in the way people view their employers; they are no longer dependent upon them for retirement and medical insurance benefits. Since investment savings and medical benefits are affordable outside of employment, people are much choosier when it comes to working for a company. This is resulting in good hiring matches based not on salaries and benefits, but instead on passion and commitment to the job itself.

The Arts

Certain art forms were traditionally very difficult to earn money from, but now artisans never have to sell actual artwork to earn money. Many artisans create videos showing how they create their art pieces, and many viewers pay to watch these videos because they too want to create that type of art, although just as many viewers are simply interested in seeing a master at work.

Starving artists are now fed by viewers from all over the world. The viewers take great pride in knowing that they are helping someone whose work they admire.

Online Video Stores

People shop online video stores just like they used to shop regular stores. Anyone can open and run an online video store. There are countless ways to present the millions of hours of videos. Video store owners (theme assemblers) collect videos they appreciate and then advertise their collections to people with similar interests and values (for example, someone interested in backpacking in Finland collects videos about where to stay, the language, cultural differences, and so on). They then add a fee layer on the videos they found helpful and advertise them to others wanting to do the same thing. They earn money whenever someone views any of the videos in their collection, even though they did not upload any videos themselves. The fee layer compensates the store owners for their efforts in offering viewers the convenience of easily finding related videos to buy.

Advertising

Advertisers have long known that consumers are interested in the opinions of other people more than the opinions of the advertisers themselves. Previously, companies would use testimonials and star ratings to show that others liked their products. Now advertisers are showcasing consumers' videos demonstrating real-life use of their products. In addition to being more cost effective for the advertisers (who essentially earn money by assembling these videos), they are getting better results from them.

For example, a stove manufacturer previously had to create an expensive commercial and buy advertising time on television. Consumers soon learned that the happy consumers shown on the commercial were actually only paid actors. Now the stove manufacturer can find and use videos that show its stove being used by actual consumers. If an uploader uploads a cooking video and tags the video with the name brand of the stove used in the video, the stove manufacturer can find this video of its stove being used and add it to its collection. People interested in purchasing a stove can visit the stove manufacturer's website and, for a few cents, watch people actually using that brand of stove, which is more powerful than paid actors dancing around the stove. The stove manufacturer is happy to know that their customers are earning money from using their product. In addition, if the stove manufacturer marks up the cost of the video for its customers, they could actually be earning money from their advertising. Crazy, huh? Earning money by advertising. This is a different world.

Charities

Charities have received so many donations that they are turning down money. They are also being questioned on their purpose and their plans for the donations they receive. Transparency regarding money is essential in all charities. It was found that many charities existed as a front for money seekers, with the hidden purpose of providing prestige and wealth to their leaders. Charities that want to end hunger in a certain area of the world, for example, need to now show how they plan to do so; if they cannot, they need to change their mission statement. Wasteful spending of donation money has been caught on video, and people no longer hand over money to charities with no questions asked.

Animal rescue charities now have the ability to upload their own videos to evidence their efforts to save abandoned and abused animals. The revenue from these videos has boosted their efforts, and many more animals are being saved from euthanasia or cruel living conditions. More importantly, these charities are combating pet over-population by offering free spay and neuter clinics in almost every community. Using their new-found video revenue, they also offer free training and dog reform schools to help pet owners manage their animals.

Impoverished areas of the world that were previously forced to rely solely on handouts from other countries are gaining independence by selling videos of life in their culture. Viewers around the globe pay to watch water and sanitation systems being installed in villages, feeling good that they are making a difference and helping to fund these humanitarian projects by simply watching the videos. This offers a never-before-seen glimpse into the lives of diverse cultures.

Not all the videos coming out of these impoverished areas focus on the typical cultural videos we have seen in the past. Videos such as "African Hut Wives" and "Indian Slum Idol" provide entertainment and help foster a level of understanding and acceptance among countries and nations. Videos that depict the core feelings and struggles humans face everywhere—family dynamics, love, death, friendship, and humor—allow people to understand that other cultures are a lot like their own.

Health

Health overall is on the rise because people are more physically active. There are no longer sickly pockets of low-income people. People have many more choices in health care now that they have the money to choose the type of care they receive; alternative and holistic treatments are used more often because people can now afford to pay for it. As before, people use caution when receiving medical attention and find horrific scenarios in both traditional health care and alternative medicines.

People place more priority on their health, and the private sector is responding and meeting this need. It is normal for people to give as much maintenance and attention to mental and physical health as they give to their physical possessions.

The Return of the Small Town

Many people are moving to small towns that were once abandoned because of their distance from high-paying jobs. These small towns offer the laid-back lifestyle and close-knit community that so many people dream about. Since more people can earn income from online videos, they are choosing to raise their families and put down roots in small towns.

As a result, small businesses that serve roughly one thousand people in a small town are also on the rise. Hardware stores, small cafes, and diners have sprung up like flowers in the spring.

Television Networks

Television networks as we knew them are gone. The networks still exist, but they have evolved into something much greater. In the old way of doing things, the networks aired only shows that advertisers would support, and shows could be canceled because of to lower viewership based on estimations provided by third-party companies. If two competing shows aired in the same timeslot, one of them was canceled. Because shows aired as new for only one time, networks depended on the gamble that the audience for that show would be able to watch it during that timeslot.

Everything is on, all the time. Networks are now known for producing high-quality shows with top performers, and they rely mostly on product placement into the stories and scenes to cover production cost. They continue to create lineups of shows as they did when they were aired over television networks, but now anyone can pay to watch them any time.

The New News

The television programs categorized as news shows have been on a downward spiral for quite some time. The news of the early twenty-first century was littered with hidden agendas, frivolous topics, and unprofessional and unbiased reporters. News networks had been constrained to show only news that was advertiser approved and appealed to the masses, which left much room for improvement.

Social separation

Money does not equal class. This has always been the rule, but now so more than ever. Just because a person has money doesn't mean he or she has class. People are drawn to other people who are similar to them in composure, values, morals, and interests.

It once was money that separated social classes. If you earned a lot of money, you were able to live in exclusive neighborhoods, attend high-ranked schools, and buy your way into high-society clubs and events. The common methods of earning money supported this class separation. It was whom you knew, where you came from, and how you acted that got you the high-paying jobs that allowed you to live in those exclusive neighborhoods and rub elbows with others just like you, and if you attended the right schools and participated in the right activities, you could land the jobs that gave you the money to buy your way out of the company of lower-class people. This was the driving force behind many dedicated workers who wanted to attend certain universities and land certain jobs so they could earn enough money to stay away from people who were not like them.

This is no longer the case. There are more and more low-class people now earning more than those highly educated people who were once at the top earning social ranking. You can be a cussin' tramp earning more than anyone else in your city and living in a bigger home than the hoity-toity echelons who once ruled.

To curb the necessity of interacting with lower-class high earners, exclusive neighborhoods and social clubs have sprung up all over that require their members to go through a screening process to allow people to connect based on interests and values, rather than just the amount of money they have.

Tourism

Since people now have more control of their time and can choose to travel whenever they want, the tourism industry has flourished like never before. Inns, bed and breakfasts, resorts, and lodges that were once considered closing their doors are prospering. Families, couples, and individuals are zigzagging across the country and around the world. Most are filming virtual vacations so their trip is paid for, turning their passions into revenue. It is now possible to get paid to travel wherever you want and to do whatever you want. Nice.

Before people travel, they can pay to watch video reviews of others who have gone before them. They learn where to go, what to do, and what to avoid, all before leaving their home. Some people film their vacations as if a viewer is sitting right next to them, which is incredible for those unable to travel because of severe physical disabilities like paraplegia. Paraplegics are now vicariously skydiving, running through jungles, climbing mountains, and camping in the wilderness.

There are many different types of virtual vacations. Some are quieter and let viewers experience the sights and sounds set to music. Other videographers talk throughout the videos as if you were right there and fill the recording with facts and up-close interactions with the locals and their cuisines, just like the Globe Trekker series. You can take a virtual vacation to anywhere in the world—Alta Vista, Iowa, population 262, or Tokyo, Japan, population 32 million. You can even purchase souvenirs; some virtual tour guides provide a link to a page where they can order some of the things they saw in gift shops or local artists' work.

Video vacations are targeted to different audiences. Some are geared toward sports fans, and some are focused on the arts.

Many people take a virtual vacation first and then visit the same location themselves. Many have traveled to small towns they would never have thought of visiting until viewing a virtual vacation. This can also be helpful for people wanting to relocate to other areas of the country.

Cities and Municipalities

Cities and municipalities learn from each other on a regular basis. Years ago a city would send a representative to another city to learn how the other city promoted itself, renovated its buildings, or set up a new software system. This method of physically sending one person across the country was a waste of taxpayers' money. Now cities and municipalities film all sorts of things so that other cities and municipalities can learn from them. People everywhere can view how one city uses its city beautification dollars to the fullest and how another decorates for the holidays or special events. They can learn how cities communicate to their citizens and how they enforce laws regarding animal leashes, jaywalking, and many other problems.

No longer are small towns struggling on their own to figure things out. They can easily watch videos from other cities similar to their own and grow together. Many cities find that they earn just as much revenue from their videos as they do from other sources. Most of the videos are accessible through a secured website, although many are open to the public.

Medical

Medical doctors have found ways to use paid videos to help their industry. Doctors are filming procedures, surgeries, and patient treatments (with the patients' consent, of course) and making the videos available within a secure website accessible only by doctors who have been granted access. Doctors around the world can now pay to watch surgeries never done before and conditions they have only read about or seen pictures of. The money doctors pay to watch the videos pays for the upfront costs incurred in filming the procedures. Many doctors hire filmmakers to shoot and edit the footage.

Small business funding

Many small business owners get their start not from bank loans, but by viewers who support their endeavors. A woman who wanted to open an art store uploaded a video showing her plan for her business, giving a tour of the building she wanted to renovate, and interviewing local artists whose work would be sold in the store. Viewers were willing to pay the slightly higher cost to view her videos because they knew she was using it to start the business. They felt proud to watch her grand opening day, knowing that they had helped make it possible.

Historic Preservation

Old buildings and homes are being renovated by viewers' support. The Carnegie Library in Superior, Wisconsin, sat partially renovated for decades while the City of Superior threatened its demolition. There was no money to complete the renovation. In an effort to raise money, friends of the library began showing photos of what it looked like in its early days. They displayed their plans to renovate it and talked about its architectural features. Viewers from around the world loved it. Never before would they have had an opportunity to see inside this building or watch the progress of its renovation. Now that it is complete and is being used as a museum, the revenue from the video views is deposited into a fund for building maintenance for decades to come. Some of the viewers felt such a connection to the building from knowing their money helped to restore such a beautiful building that they made the trip to see it in person.

Museums

Museums now earn the majority of their money from virtual video tours of their museums. The world is full of museums honoring topics from history to art forms, and online videos give viewers all over the world the chance to see things they would have never been able to see in person. People can sit in their homes and tour the great museums of the world. Many museums allow anyone visiting the museums to film videos in certain areas of the museum, keeping certain sections proprietary to their own video tours. They know that not everyone will want to watch their video tours, but allowing visitors to film parts of their collections brings attention to them. Many viewers have enjoyed the virtual tours so much that they have traveled to the museums to visit them in person.

Farmers

Farmers are no longer subsidized by the government. There is no need for them to be. People are very interested in how their food is grown and what happens on a farm, and farmers now film their own lives. People from all over the world are able to pay a few cents to watch very valuable information. Some viewers are farmers learning from another farmer, but the majority of views come from average people interested in knowing what happens on a farm. Larger companies that want to do business with farmers watch videos to get a better understanding of their customers and the challenges they face, agricultural students watch videos to learn what technology is being used, and the general population watches farmers' videos just for the fun of it. Farmers have set up field cams, barn cams, and combine cams. They're selling not only their crops or outputs, but their own lifestyles, choosing inputs, planting, weather worries, selling, and negotiations.

There are many more scenarios not presented here that could be talked about in greater detail. This is the fun part—thinking about what would change if people had the freedom to earn a living without losing control of their time. What would people do with more time and more money?

▶

CHAPTER 4

Theme Assembler 101

Theme assembler, noun: A person or business that puts together collections of similar videos.

W elcome to Theme Assembler 101. In this chapter you will learn my thoughts around the theme assembler role and why I feel it is a critical role in selling videos online.

When I search for videos online today, I often get frustrated because I cannot find a steady stream of videos that please me. If I'm looking for entertainment videos to make me laugh, only about 25 percent of the videos I find do the job. The remainder are disappointments.

When people are able to charge people to watch their videos, the inability to find videos that you actually want to purchase will either inhibit or promote purchases. Have you ever walked into a store and looked around, trying to find something to buy? You are in the mood to buy something, but there is nothing that motivates you to get out your money and make the purchase.

Imagine for a moment that there were no retail stores. If you wanted to purchase toothpaste, you would need to find manufacturers that made toothpaste and buy it directly from those manufacturers. Or consider music; imagine that you had to travel to each recording studio to buy music directly from them. This would not be efficient or a pleasurable experience.

What if there was only one kind of store that stocked all the products available? Every product that you could possibly purchase was sold in one store. There were departments, but all the departments were loaded with thousands of products that you had to look through to find what you wanted. Sometimes you would find what you were originally looking for, and sometimes you found something you didn't know existed, but when you left this enormous store with its overwhelming choices, you felt exhausted, frustrated, and unsatisfied.

Now think about your favorite store. It might be a big box store or a small, locally-owned store or boutique that stocks products you love. Imagine walking into that store and looking around. Can you feel a sense of relaxation and a sense of delight as you take in the sight of products that all seem to appeal to you? All the items offered in the store seem to be laid out especially for you. You can easily find what you want or need. You walk out of the store with the feeling that it wasn't a struggle to buy; instead, the store made it easy for you by offering a selection of products that didn't disgust or agitate you. Your shopping experience there was pleasurable, which is why you continue to return to your favorite store.

That is what a theme assembler will do. Like small shop owners, they will group together video products that appeal to you and to other customer segments. Video shoppers will have their favorite video stores, as well as some they wander into and quickly run out of.

Theme assemblers, like retailers, make shopping easy for customers because they offer similar products that appeal to specific customers and in a certain frame of mind. They mark up the prices of products to cover the cost of their efforts to create product collections and advertising.

Theme assemblers should have the ability to present any non-private video in their video collections and mark up the price, just like retailers do. Unlike retailers, theme assemblers should not be negotiating purchase prices with uploaders. To streamline the process, theme assemblers can simply select a product at its current price and add their own mark-up. When that video product is sold, the proceeds are distributed back to the theme assembler, uploader, and host company based on the original price, the mark-up, and the hosting fees.

Here is an example:

You have uploaded a video tour of your house, a recently renovated Victorian-style home on a beautiful beachfront property in Lake Geneva, Wisconsin. The price you have placed on your video is one dollar. You have titled the video "My Renovation Results," with the description, "After two years of renovations, I finally got it looking livable. Here is the tour."

You let the search engines catalogue your video with no other advertising. You set the privacy settings to allow any theme assembler to pick up the video with no restrictions. This results in about fifty views per month, earning you fifty dollars per month from that video.

Let's say I am a theme assembler with a video store of Victorian home tours. I advertise my video store in home magazines, and I use pay-per-click advertising to attract targeted customers. My site gets thousands of visitors every day from all over the world—interior designers, architects, landscapers, and home enthusiasts—all very passionate about Victorian homes.

After paying a dollar to view your video, I decide that your video will fit in my video collection. Using the theme assembler tools provided by my host company, I add your video to my collection and add a mark-up of four dollars. To better sell it, I rename the video "Beautiful Beachfront Victorian for Modern Day Living." I create my own description that is very elaborate and informs viewers they will get to see the three fireplaces, close-ups of the trim work and hardware, and the outdoor buildings. I also create a new video preview using my host company's software, focusing on parts of the video that I know will pique the interest of my customers.

Visitors to my site see the new video I added and pay five dollars to view it. The video is a hit and is purchased an average of one hundred times per day. That means you are now earning $100 a day on your video, and I am earning $400 per day (minus my host company's fees).

So what happened in this example? The theme assembler found your video (the raw product) and repackaged it to better appeal to a customer segment. This is the same thing that happens with tangible products; a marketer puts a product in appropriate packaging and presents it to the customer segments that will most likely appreciate it and purchase it.

Without the theme assembler, you earned fifty dollars per month. With the expertise of a theme assembler properly positioning your video, you earned $3,000 per month on one video. Consider the fact that your video could also be picked up by other theme assemblers packaging your video in a multitude of other ways, thereby increasing your earning potential; some other themes that could include your video could include Outstanding Beach Front Homes, Recently Renovated Homes, Homes of Wisconsin, or Lake Geneva's Beach Front Gems.

A theme assembler could boost sales of online videos exponentially if given the tools, flexibility, and options to price videos as they see fit. Theme assemblers are essential!

▶

CHAPTER 5

Videos with Potential for High Revenue

When people need to know something, they are willing to pay a price that matches the urgency or perceived value of that information at that time. Since realizing the potential revenue that videos could bring to people, I obsess about putting prices on information. As people tell me about their hobbies or my own curiosity rises during everyday meanderings, I cannot help but think what kind of video could be created for each situation and how much I would pay to view it.

It is strange that I can easily find video revenue opportunities for everyone but myself. This relates to the fact that many people downplay their own talents while easily seeing virtues in others. At Free2Earn4Ever.com you will find tools to easily show your friends and families the earning potential from their hobbies and passions. When you think of a video that someone you know could make and sell online, e-mail them the idea and the earning potential. They will appreciate it, and you will have done your good deed for the day, as my mom always says.

Videos I Would Pay To Watch

When the iPod Nano touch-screen mp3 player debuted on the market, I bought one within the first month. It did not come with a user's manual (I probably wouldn't read it anyway), nor did the online manual work. I wanted someone to show me how to use a feature called radio tag, by which I could listen to the radio and tag a song I heard so when I connected to iTunes to buy songs, the device could remind me of the songs I'd heard and wanted to own. This was a great feature for me, since I would often visit iTunes and get frustrated by not being able to find anything I wanted to buy. I had money to spend, but I couldn't find anything that motivated me to spend it. There had to be an easier way.

So there I sat, just back from Best Buy, with the little blue Nano lying there on the desk. How do I use all the fun features I know it's packed with? Straight to YouTube I went. I didn't want to read reviews about the features; I wanted to get right to the point. Tell me how to use the tag feature. I was on a mission. Come on! Why are there no videos on this feature? It just came out this month. Why am I not finding video tutorials on how to use the features?

My business mind kicked in. What is the motivation for someone who knows the Nano to put video tutorials on the web quickly? Nothing. People are busy. There was no reason for someone to post videos about the Nano so soon.

I would have paid five dollars to watch a quick, to-the-point, one-minute video on how to use the tag feature. I had just spent over $150 on the Nano, ear buds, and an iTunes card. Another five dollars for the knowledge of how to use it was nothing.

I thought about this for a moment. In today's world, time is precious. People want information, and they want it immediately. People are quite willing to pay for someone to get the point and give them the exact information they want and need at the time they need it. If I was willing to pay that much, would others around the world pay the same to watch a video? Would they pay to watch videos on other topics, too, like how to use other tech gadgets? I thought about how much a person could potentially earn from a video tutorial for an iPod Nano. If someone sold one thousand views at $5 each, it would bring in $5,000. Now, that is motivation. What other information could we be missing out on because there is no monetary motivation for people to make it available?

Another instance when I would have paid to watch a video was when my daughter dropped a dumbbell on our glass coffee table and broke the glass. I needed to order a new piece of glass, but it had to be exact. Who knows exactly what all those little lines are on a tape measure? Not me. I didn't want to place an order for glass based on what I thought a little line meant, so I went directly to YouTube to find someone who could show me how to read a tape measure. I found the perfect video. The guy in it got right to the point and didn't try to make the video longer by spouting a lot of information, like the history of the tape measure. I would gladly have paid a dollar to watch his information.

I would also pay to watch comedy videos. A few of the videos by YouTube member MrArturoTrejo are really good, and I would pay to watch them. Since I run my own business, I would pay to watch other business owners share lessons they've learned about accounting software, such as QuickBooks or Quicken. Are there other brands that I as a small business owner should know about? I would pay to have someone get to the point and tell me about stuff like that.

As I write this book and think about publishing it, I am starving for information. Books are not the best option for communicating current information because of how fast technology is changing and the different options available. There is a lot of opportunity for people who know how to do things to show others what they have learned. People don't want to reinvent the wheel, and they shouldn't have to. People need to learn from each other so we can all move forward faster as a society.

Videos that businesses should pay to watch

Businesses would be wise to watch videos of people using their products. Today they pay research firms to bring customers into focus groups or answer silly surveys in an attempt to gauge how they can improve their products or identify how customers are using their products. What if video uploaders could tag their videos with brand names and product name keywords? A company could then find videos of people using their products to see firsthand how their products are being used or how their competitors' products are being used.

When I worked in the corporate world, I watched even large corporations struggle to understand what other industries were doing. For example, if an organization builds a website, its designers first study other companies' websites. Sometimes they will schedule presentations to have another company demonstrate the behind-the-scenes factors of successful websites, although the options for such demonstrations are limited by whom they know or by names the vendor offers up as references. What if businesses could video their challenges or lessons learned and post those videos for the audience of other businesses going through the same issues? There is a lot of value in making informed choices rather than forging blindly ahead; it can often mean saving thousands of dollars that might be spent in trial and error. It would be wise for companies to share information and help each other move forward. They may find that video revenue pays for a large portion of whatever it was they were demonstrating in the video.

The New Way to Advertise

As a consumer, I like to see what products others are using. I ask friends and colleagues what products they have found to be the best. For example, I purchased a laptop about two years ago. I did a bit of research before I bought it, but I found the comments from others who'd purchased the same model to be vague and unorganized. The manufacturer and retail websites were, of course, full of flashy, professionally-made videos, none of which told me anything except how advanced, cutting edge, and great it was.

Many brands have fanatics—people who are in love with the brand. They talk about a certain branded product as if it were their own. They enjoy telling anyone willing to listen about how great the products are, and you can see the excitement in their eyes. What if they could shoot videos of why the product is so great and what they are doing with it, and sell that video online?

Of course, some people do this already. However, I am suggesting that companies use these brand fanatics' videos on their own sites in addition to the flashy, professionally-made videos. Consumers are wise to the actors and celebrity endorsers who get paid to sell a product but don't actually use it. Using authentic videos will help sell products, and as a bonus, the brand fanatics earn money when a potential consumer watches their videos.

There are many people who buy products and then want to know how to use them. Companies should post video tutorials on their websites, because people really want to learn from each other. They want to avoid making costly mistakes with time or money. Paying a few cents before or even after purchasing an item to watch how someone else is using that item is a wise investment in many instances.

Some products have user groups where users of a particular product share information about how they use a product. Add money to the mix, and you will have higher participation, better quality conversations, and a boosted economy, because more people will be participating in the core economic activities—earning and spending.

Film Makers, Actors, Comedians

The entertainment business is huge. Unfortunately, you can either make it big or not make it at all by having to still work another job to earn money. When I was young, my mom and I talked about the lottery and the huge sums of money people won. She said, "Why do they give it all to one person? Can't they spread it around a bit more? Instead of one person getting that much, give smaller amounts to more people."

Apply that same concept to the entertainment industry. Why does it have to be a feast or famine industry? You're either entertaining an arena or waiting tables. It is not right. We need to let more people play. Now is the time. I feel I am missing out on entertainment that could bring joy to my soul. You know the euphoric feeling you get when you laugh so hard you start to cry, or that moving storyline that tugs at your heart strings? Our world is full of people who can move us through entertainment, but they are too busy working their day jobs to have time to write a great script or coordinate a film, especially since the odds of earning any money from their efforts are slim. So we miss out. It's sad.

MrArturoTrejo, the YouTube member I mentioned previously, created the interview with a one-year-old that I referenced above, which I find hugely funny. If I watch it in the right mood, I cry from laughing so hard. It's similar to the hula chair video. Hilarious! In his more recent videos, MrArturoTrejo mentions that he is busy at work and hasn't had time to create the videos he would like. I feel like I'm missing out. He is very talented, but because he does not have the ability to earn the money he should earn through his videos, he has to work another job.

How many other extremely talented individuals are too busy working the job that pays them to use their God-given talents to make people laugh or cry? This is not the case solely in the entertainment industry, either; it impacts every aspect of our lives. Busied hands are not free.

▶

CHAPTER 6

Why Would Viewers Pay to Watch Videos When There are Free Videos Available?

As I told people about my idea, a common question emerged: Why would people pay to watch videos when the videos out there today are free? Time and time again this question came up. At first it irritated me that people could not understand why when the reasons were so clear to me.

Imagine for a moment, the conversations that must have happened when someone in a soda bottling company came up with the crazy idea to sell bottled water. The same question would have been fired back at that idea. Why would anyone pay for a bottle of water when they can get water from the tap for free? Fast forward to today, in the United States alone, bottled water sales have exceeded $30 billion annually.

My response to those asking this question was usually a myriad of thought provoking questions. Why do people buy books when they can check them out free from the library? Why do people buy bottled water when it is free from the tap? Why would someone pay for valet parking, when they can go park it themselves? Have you put any videos out on YouTube yet? Why not? What is your motivation, right? Now, what if I told you that if you put a video out there you could earn a few hundred dollars from that video? Does that change your mind about putting a video out there?

There are three main reasons why people will pay to watch videos online:

Convenience
Value perception –low price
Unique content

Convenience

People have shown that they pay for convenience. Valet parking, bottled water, rush order fees, are just a few examples. In an age where we demand instant gratification, we are willing to pay. When I purchased my iPod Nano Touch, for convenience, I would have willingly paid $5 for someone to show me how to use the radio tagging feature. When time is money, and so many of us with our busy lives have pushed the value of time to an all time high. For someone that has all the time in the world to find answers and research things, they may not perceive a high dollar value for their time. On the other side of the spectrum, someone who is extremely busy and rushed where time is hurried, time has a whole new value.

Value perception – low price

Value perception is a science in and of itself. Look at what people in our US society put value on. When I say value, I mean what they willing to pay for items whose cost to manufacture is extremely low in comparison to the sale price. Brand name items are a perfect example. There are handbags, clothes, and shoes that because they have a brand name on them have people going into debt to purchase them.

Information is power. Information is knowledge. Information in its purest form is undervalued. In the show Seinfeld, there is scene where Elaine is trying to find the quickest way to the airport. She explains to Jerry that some homeless guy gave me the directions, but he made me pay him $5.

The homeless guy is smart. To earn money, he sells what he has...information.

Unique Content

Large audiences are what most television networks look at when determining what types of programs they offer. Book publishers to, look at the potential reader market before signing an author. When there is a large enough group of willing buyers, then information and products are created to meet those groups.

There is another layer of opportunity that is being pursued today called niche marketing. This basically means you have smaller groups of buyers that have a similar need. An example of niche is a clothing line for hamsters. Not a lot of people purchase them, but there are people that purchase them.

Selling videos online would meet the mass market and the niche marketing, and even a more granular level. Videos could have personalized information for tiny segments of people. Possibly one to 100 people and these are segments where publishing a book or creating a product may not be profitable where a video could be.

▶

CHAPTER 7

"Sell the sizzle, not the steak."

-unknown

Features and Benefits

For many years, I worked in the corporate environment, creating web applications that met users' needs. To this day, my mind is always in problem solving mode. How can we harness technology to solve problems, make life easier, and do things most efficiently? In this chapter you will get a glimpse of how I connect the dots. I often brainstorm about how to utilize existing technologies or ideas to make online video sales a very lucrative option for many.

The examples in this chapter contain some amusing stories illustrating how these features can be used in real-life scenarios. When the author of a book tries to be cute in his or her writing, it can either irritate me or entertain me, depending upon my mood. Sometimes I am in a more serious mood, and any quirky writing style irks me so that I want to stop reading the book or skip ahead through the pages because I feel that these little reading adventures are a waste of my time.

Core Global Features

Core global features are the features that must be present for this to work as I envision it. We'll get to the super fun features later on in the chapter.

Video Identification Numbers

Feature Description: Every video should have a system-generated video identification number (VIN) so that uploaders can advertise their videos and ensure that viewers can navigate directly to specific videos. This VIN would be similar to a product's UPC code. When a theme assembler adds someone else's video to his or her collection, the video would get its own unique VIN linked to the theme assembler. This allows one video to be referred to by two different VINs. If the theme assembler wants advertise that video, he or she wants to make sure that paying viewers go directly to his marked-up copy of the video, not the original uploader's version. If a video had only one VIN that had to be shared by both the uploader and the theme assembler, the paying viewer would choose to watch the video with the lowest price.

Benefit to Viewer: With video identification numbers in place, there will be no difficulty in finding a video. Viewers need only enter the exact VIN to find the intended video, making it simple and easy to make the purchase.

Benefit to Uploader or Theme Assembler: Uploaders and theme assemblers can be confident that viewers will be able to easily find the intended video. They will also have the ability to incorporate VINs into print media—magazines, newspapers, website copy, billboards, products, etc.—and drive viewers directly to the video.

Benefit to Host Company: Video identification numbers will result in higher revenue for host companies because user satisfaction will be higher. More uploaders and theme assemblers will advertise their videos because they know viewers can be sure to find their video, which will result in higher revenues.

Example of Feature in Use: Flipping through the latest edition of the *This Old House* magazine, I come to the last page where a house in need of repair is featured. At the bottom of the article is a video identification number. I visit the website of the host company listed in the magazine or, better yet, my favorite search engine, type the video identification number into the search, and receive a whole collection of videos about this house. The videos each cost a few cents to watch, but by watching them I get a walk-through tour of the home. I can choose from videos that focus on the trim work, the hardware, the exterior, and many other areas of the home. It is a much more satisfying experience than just reading the article.

Example 2: You are a theme assembler and have just put together the best collection of skateboarding videos ever. You searched for days to compile the perfect videos. All the videos you found were priced at a dollar by the uploaders, and when you added them to your collection, you marked up each price by two dollars, which means your collection now contains the best collection of skateboarding videos at three dollars each. You then purchase an advertisement in the *California Skateboarding* magazine, referencing in your ad the video identification number for your gnarly videos. When skateboarders see your ad, they can enter your video identification number in a search engine to find your collection of videos.

Preview Maker

Feature Description: Video uploaders could use the preview maker feature to easily create a video preview for potential viewers to watch before deciding to buy a video. Uploaders use a slider to select certain scenes from the beginning, middle, and end of a video to create the preview. This would prevent the uploader from selecting only the first few seconds of the video, which may not accurately reflect the contents of the entire video. Theme assemblers and uploaders should have the ability to create their own variations of previews for the same video.

Benefit to Viewer: This feature will provide viewers the opportunity to see what they will be buying.

Benefit to Uploader or Theme Assembler: This easy global feature will enable uploaders and theme assemblers to create a preview without expensive editing software.

Example of Feature in Use: A ten-minute video is uploaded demonstrating how to change the blade on a Toro 2033 lawnmower. The uploader uses the preview maker to easily select small segments from the beginning, middle, and end of the video to create a preview. Once the video is uploaded, viewers watch the preview to get a glimpse of the information the video will cover, how well it is presented, and the quality of the audio and lighting. Based on the preview and other factors, viewers decide to purchase the video.

Video Description

Feature Description: Uploaders could type in a description of what their videos are about. Theme assemblers could add their own descriptions of the same videos and choose whether or not to show the uploader's description.

Benefit to Viewer: Viewers will know what a video is about before purchasing it.

Benefit to Uploader or Theme Assembler: Uploaders can describe what takes place in a video, and theme assemblers can add their own descriptions based on how they plan to present it for sale in their stores.

Benefit to Host Company: Multiple descriptions attract more viewers of varied types, and more purchases result in increased revenue.

Example of Feature in Use: A lady uploads a video of her pug licking her baby's face. Her description of the video reads, "Tug the pug kissing baby Andrew." A theme assembler sees the video and includes it in his collection of videos illustrating how animals make people sick. His description of the video reads, "See how this lady is oblivious to the transfer of E. coli and other fecal bacteria into her baby's mouth."

Star Reviews

Feature Description: Viewers will be able to rate a video they watched by giving it a certain number of stars. Ratings given by viewers who watched the video as part of a theme assembler's collection are kept separate from ratings received by other theme assemblers and the original uploader. Read the example to see why this separation is necessary.

Benefit to Viewer: Viewers can easily see the popularity of a video.

Benefit to Uploader or Theme Assembler: By keeping ratings separated by uploader and theme assembler, ratings will provide feedback on how each one presented the video, which could be very different.

Example of Feature in Use: An uploader posts a video of a boy skateboarding, presenting it as praise for the child's advanced tricks for his age. People read the uploader's description, purchase the video, and rate it based on how it was presented to them.

The same video is picked up by a theme assembler, who describes the video as boys dressed like dorks and markets the video to an audience wanting to know what kids like to wear. Viewers that watch the video and focus on the clothes may rate the video differently from those who watched it to see the cool tricks.

Privacy Options

Feature Description: Uploaders will be able to choose whether or not videos appear in search results, can be picked up by theme assemblers, or appear only within username- and password-protected websites.

Benefit to Viewer: Since uploaders can make videos available to only certain viewers, uploaders feel comfortable selling videos they don't want the whole world to see.

Benefit to Uploader or Theme Assembler: Uploaders can prevent theme assemblers from using their videos and can also control where and how their videos appear.

Benefit to Host Company: More videos will be hosted because of the privacy options.

Example of Feature in Use: A password-protected research website for use only by brain surgeons sells videos of brain surgeries or researchers addressing brain surgeons regarding the latest research. Websites such as these can show videos not intended for the general public.

Example 2: A club's website sells videos for club members only, available solely by direct link. This means that the club's videos would not be included in any search results, nor would they be available to theme assemblers.

Money Exchange

Feature Description: Since ease of purchase sells more products, viewers' ability to easily purchase a video is essential. There should be only one click required to exchange money among viewers, uploaders, theme assemblers, and host companies. The monetary exchange process should also automatically convert prices and funds into other currencies in order to allow international purchases.

Benefit to Viewer: Viewers can easily purchase videos from other countries without having to give thought to currency exchange.

Benefit to Uploader or Theme Assembler: Uploaders and theme assemblers are able to sell videos internationally, resulting in the opportunity for more revenue.

Benefit to Host Company: Currency converters will also provide host companies more opportunities for transactions, resulting in higher revenue.

Example of Feature in Use: A Japanese family creates videos of what life is like after an earthquake, and people from all over the world can purchase their videos. The host company automatically displays the cost of the video in each viewer's local currency. When a viewer pays for the video, the host company pays the Japanese family in their own currency, based on exchange rates at the time of purchase. This allows for international sales without currency exchange hurdles for uploaders, viewers, or theme assemblers.

Verified Services Provided by Host Companies

Feature Description: For an additional fee, uploaders can have their host company confirm that video descriptions and categorizations are standard and accurate.

Benefit to Viewer: Viewers can be confident that descriptions, keywords, ratings, and tagging are accurate, according to each host company's standards.

Benefit to Uploader or Theme Assembler: As theme assemblers set their search filters, they can choose to view only verified videos, eliminating the chance that videos will be improperly represented.

Benefit to Host Company: Verification would be a paid service that will earn more revenue for host companies.

Example of Feature in Use: A mom sets up a search filter for her five-year-old son that allows only videos rated for general audiences that have been verified they are rated appropriately. She now feels confident that someone besides the uploader has properly rated the videos her son will find.

Search Filters

Feature Description: Viewers and theme assemblers can use search filters to find videos that meet certain criteria, such as geographic location, date of creation or upload, keywords, star rating, number of views, price range, audience rating, verification status, and tags, among other.

Benefit to Viewer: Viewers can narrow search results to find more relevant videos, resulting in higher likelihood of purchasing.

Benefit to Uploader or Theme Assembler: More relevant videos will appear in search results more often and match what viewers are looking for.

Benefit to Host Company: Search filters create better user experiences for all roles.

Example of Feature in Use: I create a search filter for videos filmed in Finland in the last month that are rated for general audiences, cost less than a dollar, and include an authentic Finnish sauna. The search results will show only videos that meet all my selected criteria, eliminating the frustration of having to browse through pages of irrelevant videos. I can find the video I want in a shorter time and am more likely to purchase it because it meets my need at that time.

Content Rating

Feature Description: A content rating scale will be needed, similar to that use for television shows and video games, to determine whether video content is appropriate for certain audiences. Uploaders can put a content rating on their videos and can pay to have their content ratings verified by their host companies.

If an uploader rates a video for general audiences and pays the additional fee to have the rating verified, the host company will review the video to confirm whether or not the uploader's rating is correct according to general guidelines. If the host company rates the differently, viewers see both ratings in the video detail information. Viewers can then use both ratings as determining factors when deciding whether or not to buy the video.

Benefit to Viewer: Content ratings help parents and others sensitive to certain content control the type of videos that appear in search results. Viewers would never see videos that contain offensive content, thereby avoiding any danger of accidentally witnessing vulgar content.

Benefit to Uploader or Theme Assembler: Uploaders and theme assemblers can use ratings to target specific audiences.

Example of feature in use: If you want to find stand-up comedy videos appropriate for your cousins ages five and six, you can set a search filter to show only videos rated G for general audiences to view search results that are age appropriate.

Global Filters for Viewers

Feature Description: Viewers can apply global filters to all searches performed from their accounts, to allow them to always see only videos that meet those search criteria.

Benefit to Viewer: With global search filters set, viewers need never see videos that disgust them, increasing their comfort level with purchasing online videos.

Benefit to Host Company: Host companies will be able to serve more audience segments without tarnishing viewers' perceptions of the quality of video content.

Example of Feature in Use: Parents will be able to set global filters for their children's accounts to block videos from other countries or videos with content ratings other than G. When the children search for videos, only videos that meet the specified criteria would appear in results. As children visit other websites and found videos for sale, they can only purchase videos that align with the global filter set for their account.

It is possible that the majority of videos hosted by certain host companies are designed for adults and rated for people over age fourteen due to the subject matter. However, with the help of global filters, audiences disgusted by these types of videos will never have to never see those videos. This will keep viewers' perception of online video purchases cleaner. It is like hanging a curtain around a room of adult videos. Children and anyone not interested in those titles will never be subject to them.

Playlists

Feature Description: Uploaders and theme assemblers can set up playlists of videos that can be purchased as a bundle.

Benefit to Viewer: Viewers can easily purchase groups of videos that stay grouped as a playlist. They won't be forced to purchase the entire playlist; they can purchase one or a few of the videos in a playlist.

Benefit to Uploader or Theme Assembler: Playlists allow uploaders and theme assemblers more options when presenting videos for sale. This feature keeps videos together for a better presentation to potential viewers.

Example of Feature in Use: A theme assembler who specializes in daily laughs and markets videos as "morning coffee for your funny bone" groups together short, hilarious videos that never exceed ten minutes time as a group. He finds five two-minute videos and creates a playlist from them. His host company's playlist feature allows viewers to purchase the entire playlist at the same cost if they wish, rather than having to purchase each video individually. Viewers can also purchase playlists and send them to others as gifts.

Comment Restrictions

Feature Description: Uploaders and theme assemblers can set restrictions on comments left by viewers. For example, comments can be restricted to paying viewers only instead of any users that come along and preview the video. Comments can be restricted to allow only one post per viewer, eliminating the back-and-forth bickering that can occur. Commenting can also be turned off completely, not allowing anyone to post a comment about a video. Similar to the star rating feature, comments from viewers watching a video as presented by a theme assembler are kept separate from viewer comments received from the uploader.

Benefit to Viewer: Viewers can see other viewers' comments related to the video as it was presented to them. Viewers also can have their comments restricted to only one post so it completely eliminates the back and forth bickering that can happen among viewers posting comments.

Benefit to Uploader or Theme Assembler: Keeping comments separate allows theme assemblers and uploaders to adjust comment restrictions independently of one another.

Example of Feature in Use: A knitting club consisting of men making hats for their wives creates a series of videos showing men how to knit while still looking manly. The club uses marketing activities to unite knitting men all over the globe. The club limits comments on their videos to paid viewers only and allows only one comment per viewer.

The members of the club want to make their wives wildly exotic hats made from the most rare and expensive yarn in the world, so they charge five dollars to view their videos in order to help pay for the yarn. Realizing that theme assemblers could help boost video sales, they allow any theme assembler to pick up their videos.

One theme assembler is interested in the art of knitting. She adds the club's videos into her collection and marks up the videos anywhere from six to eight dollars per view. Meanwhile, another theme assembler adds the videos to his collection of "girly men doing girly things," sets the price at seven dollars per view, and markets them to people looking for a laugh. This theme assembler wants comments back and forth between viewers, making it a communal activity to make fun of the knitters, so the theme assembler allows unlimited comments from all viewers.

Since the comments are kept separate, the men seriously interested in knitting hats for their wives who view the videos from the club's site or the store owned by the theme assembler truly interested in knitting would not be exposed to the derogatory comments from people making fun of the guys.

See the privacy options feature for more details on how uploaders can choose the theme assemblers who can sell their videos.

Super Fun Features

Super fun features are, well, super fun, or funner, as I like to say. The following features aren't crucial but would make online video sales much better for all the roles.

GPS Tagging

Feature Description: When a video is uploaded to a host company's site, the uploader can specify the geographic location where a video was filmed. The viewer can then use a special app to find videos within a certain range of a certain location at any given time.

Benefit to Viewer: Viewers are able to find relevant videos at any given location in the world.

Benefit to Uploader or Theme Assembler: GPS tagging gives uploaders and theme assemblers the ability to present videos to people who are more likely to be interested in them because of their location, such as walking tours and event or incident coverage. Creativity abounds with this feature.

Benefit to Host Company: As videos are targeted to more audiences, more sales increase.

Example of Feature in Use: A college student has just moved into a new dorm. He checks his Video Locator app to see if any videos are available that were filmed in his dorm. He comes across party videos, heads up videos from other students, walking tours, and videos recommending the best places to eat. The videos cost a few cents each, but they are incredibly helpful to a new student like himself. It is like having a guide show him around.

Meanwhile, the uploaders are earning party money from every student who views their videos.

Example 2: A family of four goes on vacation in Hawaii, taking a break from the cold Michigan winter. The kids are bored on this $10,000 vacation—imagine that! What should they do for the remainder of the day? Check the app. With the help of GPS tagging, they can watch videos of people doing all kinds of activities in the very location in which they are standing. It is like an instant tour guide, a travel brochure, and a "been there, done that" veteran combined.

Pay-To-Watch Live Video

Feature Description: Uploaders can sell live (real-time) videos. Think *The Truman Show.*

Benefit to Viewer: Viewers will have access to live video of a multitude of subjects. There is something different about watching something happen live, right now, instead of a video shot at an earlier time. It often carries more impact if you can watch it as it happens.

Benefit to Uploader or Theme Assembler: Uploaders will find joy in giving other people the opportunity to experience what they are seeing in real time. Theme assemblers have the option to present collections of live videos to viewers.

Benefit to Host Company: Since hosting live video involves a different process from pre-recorded footage, host companies may charge a higher host fee percentage on live video.

Example of Feature in Use: Boxing matches have sold live video coverage of events dating back to the early 1980s, but people will pay to watch many other subjects live besides sporting events. For example, nature can put on some spectacular shows, not only with animal behaviors, but also with weather and natural disasters.

As a tornado rips through a town, leveling buildings and changing the landscape forever, people can receive their own aid by letting the world see their pain and trials of experiencing nature's fury up close. As long as uploaders retain access to Internet, the eyes of the world can pay to watch from different live streaming videos around the town, getting up-close views of the wreckage, hearing the trembling voices of those who survived, and seeing areas that typical news crews could never cover in one day. After the news crews have gone on to another story, those still interested in the aftermath can continue to pay to watch live footage, knowing the money they pay to watch this footage is going directly to those who need it most and, more importantly, those they choose to pay to watch.

Example 2: African villages situated among wildlife the rest of the world thinks of as exotic can show live video of the animals living in their natural surroundings rather than in cages. Perched atop a tall tree, a live video tower can film lions capturing prey and the migration of large herds of animals, all available for the world to pay to watch. The money brought in from these videos helps bring an economic rebirth to this area like it has never experienced before as the village earns money from undisturbed nature at its wildest, something the village knows to protect and be thankful for.

Gifting Options

Feature Description: Availability for a viewer to purchase a video or playlist of videos and send it electronically to someone else for viewing free of charge.

Benefit to Viewer: Get online videos as gifts! These videos may contain information you've been looking for but haven't been able to find.

Benefit to Uploader or Theme Assembler: More options to market videos to viewers.

Benefit to host company: More sales equal more revenue.

Example of Feature in Use: Your friend has just been diagnosed with a rare disorder. To help out, you start searching for videos of people with the same disorder, looking specifically for cures. You find a collection of 150 videos of someone with the same disorder. You watch a few of the previews and select ten of the videos to purchase for your friend. Your friend receives a message from you with the videos. He sends them to his television and watches them with his family. Your friend calls you, so excited and grateful for the videos you sent, to thank you for the hope you gave him.

Example 2: How many times have you come across an online video and thought of people you know would enjoy it? Or have you frantically searched for the perfect gift for someone but been unsuccessful in finding a tangible product to purchase? Now you have millions of possible gift choices.

Storefronts

Feature Description: Storefronts provide theme assemblers a platform to manage their own online video stores. Under their profiles they can create multiple stores and drive traffic to those stores using video identification numbers.

Benefit to Viewer: Viewers have the convenience of video collections presented for easy browsing and buying.

Benefit to Uploader or Theme Assembler: Storefronts would create more options to market videos to viewers.

Benefit to Host Company: More sales equal more revenue.

Example of Feature in Use: When planning your first trip to Paris, you can visit a storefront that contains all the videos relevant to you as a traveler to this foreign city—preparing proper documentation, language musts, hotel reviews, walking tours, things to watch out for, and so on. Instead of using a search filter to try to find all these videos on your own, storefronts enable you to easily find the videos you will need for a successful trip, in a fraction of the time and without frustration.

Music Store

Feature Description: As an uploader edits a video with the host company's editing program, he or she can add background music from the host company's Music Store by simply clicking "add music" and then finding songs, instrumental-only songs, and sound effects to add to the video.

Independent musicians and record companies could add their music to the store and set a price for uploaders to incorporate it into their videos, as well as setting the price for viewers to purchase each song for the one-click-music-buy feature.

When uploaders find songs they want to add to their videos, they select the songs, pay for them, and incorporate them into their videos using the host company's editing program. By doing this, uploaders are legally incorporating music into their videos, which also makes those songs conveniently available to viewers to purchase the songs used in the video.

Benefit to Viewer: Viewers have access to better videos with music and sound effects.

Benefit to Uploader or Theme Assembler: Music stores create easy options to legally incorporate music into videos to create a more engaging and enjoyable viewing experience.

Benefit to Music Artists and Recording Companies: Music producers have the opportunity to make their music available for use in videos, which increases exposure to their music and gives viewers access to one-click-music-buy, which means selling more music.

Example of Feature in Use: A group of six neighborhood kids ages seven to ten years old loves to put on musical plays for their neighbors, creating story lines and popular music scenes with choreographed dances. The neighbors gather in a mock theater of plastic lawn chairs to watch the kids put on the play while one of the dads videotapes it. The kids then use a host company's editing program to create a great video from the recording, adding sound effects and using the recorded versions of the songs.

Example 2: An aspiring singer living in the projects of southern Philadelphia can belt out songs like the professionals. He sometimes sits on street corners and sings because he enjoys it so much. Everyone tells him he is just as good as the people singing on the radio. It's too bad he can't get discovered and leave the ghetto. His phone has a video camera on it, so he sets it up and sings a few Top 40 songs. He visits the library to upload the video to the Internet. Using a video editing program, he finds the instrumental versions of the songs he sang and adjusts them to play in the background of his video. He uploads the edited videos to the Internet and waits. A few days later, his video is picked up by a theme assembler, and the text alerts he set for his videos report that his videos have gone viral, earning fifty cents per video at one million views. He sings out with joy!

One-Click-Music-Buy

Feature Description: When a viewer previews or purchases a video, a music note icon links them to a page where all the songs used in that video can be purchased.

Benefit to Viewer: It is easy to purchase songs heard in a video. The music can be bought immediately, without having to navigate to a different site to find the songs.

Benefit to Uploader or Theme Assembler: Uploaders have the ability to produce better videos with music incorporated into them.

Benefit to Host Company: One-click-music-buy generates more sales and revenue.

Example of Feature in Use: You have signed up to participate in a local marathon and want to figure out how to train properly. You find a video about someone training for the Manhattan marathon and giving nutrition tips. In the video you hear the *Rocky* theme song "Gonna Fly Now," "Let's Get It Started" by the Black Eyed Peas, and "Kryptonite" by 3 Doors Down. You are pumped and ready to train! You click the music note icon at the bottom of the video, and in one click you can purchase any or all of the songs that were included in that video.

Example 2: In two months you are hosting a dinner party, and you'd like to class it up a bit. You find a video about how to host a high-society dinner party that shows table settings, hiring a caterer, greeting guests, and etiquette, as well as what types of music to play. The video host explains how to hire Best Buy to install a whole-house music system and recommends a few songs. The host also states that he or she has selected five hours of music to play during the night. You click the music note icon, and in one click you are able to purchase all five hours of pre-selected music that will be perfect for your dinner party.

Brand Tagging and Product Buy

Feature Description: Uploaders can select brands of products used in their videos and tag those brands to help garner search results to match more accurately what viewers are looking for. Companies selling products can register all their products into a product database for exact matching. They can also provide a URL link to a site that gives viewers the opportunity to purchase or get additional information on the product found in the video. Viewers can search based on exact product names and click a "product buy" button to buy the actual product from the manufacturer.

Benefit to Viewer: Viewers have the ability to find videos on exact products. More videos are available because product owners are now more likely to produce videos of their products in order to earn revenue from their videos.

Benefit to Uploader or Theme Assembler: Uploaders have more opportunities to sell videos reviewing products, and theme assemblers have more videos to choose from to assemble in relevant themes.

Benefit to Host Company: Host companies earn higher commission revenue from sales made through the Product Buy feature.

Example of Feature in Use: Your vacuum cleaner no longer generates suction. That sucks! Now you need to buy a new one. You've been thinking of the Dyson DC41 Animal, but you've also considered the Oreck XL Element. You use the Product Exact Search feature and select these two vacuums, returning search results of over one thousand videos. Your narrow your search to include only your state, verified videos, video running times of less than ten minutes, and prices less than one dollar. You now have only fifty videos to choose from. You scroll through the list and watch a few of the videos. After watching actual customers demonstrate the vacuums in their own homes, you find the one you want to buy and click on the shopping cart icon, which sends you directly to a site that sells the model you want. All you have to do is click the purchase button, and in less than a minute, a new vacuum is on its way to you. Shopping this way gives you a look at the product in use by actual customers, not paid actors, and the money you spent watching the videos is offset by the time you saved. In addition, you've also learned how to use many of the product's features just by watching other people use it.

Example 2: You are building a new house and will be meeting with your general contractor in a week to discuss the electrical features you want included in the house. You've been thinking about environment-friendly ways to incorporate lights and sound into your home, so with a *Green Builder* magazine in hand, you start searching videos of products profiled in the magazine. You can now see how other people have incorporated these products into their homes and determine what you like. You can also hear directly from homeowners about how satisfied they are with the products and what they would have done differently. With the cost of building a new home, spending a few hundred dollars on research is a good investment to ensure your building decisions are ones you will not regret.

Charity Select

Feature Description: When uploaders determine what bank accounts they want the revenue for particular videos to go into, they have the option to put a percentage of any revenue toward a charity. Charities can register their organizations in host com-

panies' databases and provide bank information so that uploaders can easily send revenue their way. When uploaders select the
option to donate revenue to a charity, they are then presented
with a list of verified charities. They then select the percentage
of revenue they wish to be donated to the charity they choose.
When a viewer looks at a video and considers purchasing it,
the viewer can see that a percentage of all the revenue earned
from that video goes to a particular charity or multiple charities, although uploaders have the option of not displaying the
charities they have chosen.

Benefit to Viewer: Viewers can easily see what charities they will
be supporting by purchasing specific videos.

Benefit to Uploader or Theme Assembler: Uploaders and theme
assemblers have the ability to funnel revenue directly to favorite
charities.

Example of Feature in Use: I create a video about how I set up
record keeping for my business. After I upload the video, I then
select where I want the revenue from this video to go. I put 20
percent of the revenue in my savings account, 40 percent into a
savings account for my daughter, 30 percent to Second Chance
Animal Rescue of Minnesota (where I adopted one of my dogs.)

Example 2: You visit your favorite charity's website. From their video store, you can purchase all different types of videos from people all over the world who have allocated a percentage of the videos' revenues to that charity. It makes you feel good that you can purchase videos for entertainment and education while helping out your favorite charities.

Theme Assemblers' Dynamic Video Stores

Feature Description: Theme assemblers can create a dynamic page where videos that meet particular criteria would automatically be added to or deleted from their store. Theme assemblers can also set qualifying videos to auto display or pending display, to make videos immediately available as they meet the criteria for that section of the theme assembler's store or to be placed in a pending group waiting for manual approval from the theme assembler before becoming available for sale in the store. Theme assemblers could put filters on videos and make the same filters available to viewers.

Benefit to Viewer: Viewers are treated to continually fresh videos populating their favorite theme assemblers' dynamic video stores.

Benefit to Uploader or Theme Assembler: Uploaders can take advantage of technology and have their videos quickly picked up by theme assemblers wanting to display that type of video.

Example of Feature in Use: A theme assembler sets up a dynamic video store to sell electric car reviews. He sets up different areas of the store for different types of cars and establishes search criteria for each section. As videos meeting these criteria are uploaded, they are automatically added to his store. Viewers know they can visit his store to find the latest videos pertaining to electric car reviews, eliminating the need for extensive searching.

CHAPTER 8

"Remembering that you are going to die is the best way I know to avoid the trap of thinking you have something to lose."

-Steve Jobs

Make It Happen

Results happen because of action. Let's start a global conversation about this idea. Your action could start a revolution that will change the way people live—a revolution that would give people all over the world the ability to earn money from their God-given talent, their experiences, and their knowledge. How freeing that would be!

With the economy in the tank, people are working themselves to death, with no time to enjoy life, no time for their families, and perhaps no time to even start a family. We need this freedom to earn now more than ever. We as a society have become so accustomed to the way things are that many have shut out the possibility of finding freedom, happiness, and joy. The Free 2 Earn idea is what people have been praying about and begging for.

This idea is not one you read about and forget soon after. Opportunity has been presented. It is up to you to take action to make this happen, if not for you, for the people you care about and the ones you see struggling. Consider what talents, skills, or experiences they could put in an online video that could bring them revenue for years to come.

Find at least three things on the list of actions below and commit to doing them this week. If you are really inspired, do all of them. Don't hesitate or procrastinate. The payoff for these few actions is huge!

1. **Get a calculator**, visit an online video site like YouTube that displays the number of views for each video, and start doing some conservative math to understand the impact of this idea. Take a good look at the number of views these videos are getting. Let's say that once people start charging a fee to view a video, only 20 percent of the people who watch a video today would actually purchase that video. This will give you an idea of how much people could earn. When people earn, people spend. It gets the economy moving.

2. **Use our Free 2 Earn 4 Ever Revenue Projection Calculator.** We have created a calculator at our Website, www.Free2Earn4Ever.com, that you can use to research earning potential from videos. When you tell others about Free 2 Earn 4 Ever, refer them to the online calculator so they too can see the earning potential.

3. **Tell everyone you know about this idea.** As you go about your day, stop and tell people about the idea. Refer them to our website, www.Free2Earn4Ever.com.

   If you use Twitter, tweet it, not once, but periodically. Link to Free2Earn4Ever.com. If you have a Facebook account, post it on your wall and like our Facebook page. On LinkedIn or other career networking sites, post a status update that you've read the Free 2 Earn 4 Ever book and are excited about the possibilities.

If you already post videos online, create a video telling your viewers about this idea and ask them to post a comment about how much they would pay to watch some of your videos. Be the person they hear this idea from. When you hear a message of hope, you always remember who you heard it from first.

If you blog, blog about the possibilities that Free 2 Earn 4 Ever could bring, not once, but every so often. Think about intriguing questions you can pose to your blog followers. What impact could selling online videos have on your industry? What new opportunities could be uncovered? What online videos would your blog fans pay to watch? If your blog turned into a vlog, ask your fans how much they would pay to watch your vlogs. Enter the figures they give you into the Free 2 Earn 4 Ever calculator to calculate how much you could possibly earn from paid vlogging. Does it surpass what you are making from ad revenue sharing?

Start a discussion group to discuss this book and to get people talking about what this idea could do for the economy—for their economy, for your local economy, and for local charities. What does your town, school, or organization need money for? What types of videos could you sell online to bring in revenue to purchase what you need? Use the calculator at www.Free2Earn-4Ever.com to find out how many videos and views you would need to reach your goal.

4. **The power of the pen** or typed word. Write a letter to the top technology companies and let them know you want this. Tell them to bring this to life. Tell them why it is important to you and explain how your life would change if you had the ability to sell your online videos. There are letter templates you can print at www.Free2Earn4Ever.com.

Technology companies will not be able to ignore the public's desire to get this started. The tech companies listed below are top in the industry, and they are currently using the technology that selling online videos will require. Companies are successful because they can meet consumer needs, and many companies pay research firms to watch consumer trends. Tell them directly what you want. The louder the voice, the quicker the action. I anticipate that some of these companies will state that it is too risky to take on because of legal aspects, but I believe that is simply not true. Yes, there will be legal issues to work through; however, anything is possible. Imagine mail carts full of letters from people all over the world arriving at the addresses below, asking that these companies provide the tools for *anyone* to sell a video about *anything* (as long as it's legal, of course).

Google
1600 Amphitheatre Parkway
Mountain View, CA 94043

YouTube, LLC
901 Cherry Ave
San Bruno, CA 94066

PayPal USA Corporation Office Headquarters
2211 North First Street
San Jose, CA 95131

Apple
1 Infinite Loop
Cupertino, CA 95014

Amazon.com HQ
1200 12th Ave S. #1200
Seattle, WA 98144

5. **E-mail or write a letter to your political representatives** to let them know you want this. Tell them that if we the people are given the tools, we can fix the economy ourselves, although there is much work on the government's part to reign in their spending to align better with our economy at any given time. Tell them that it is earning and spending that get an economy moving, not jobs. Jobs are only one way people can earn. The Free 2 Earn 4 Ever plan would give so many more people an opportunity to earn money for themselves than jobs ever could. Besides, more jobs will only directly help those in need of a job. What about those struggling who already have jobs? Jobs will come naturally as people start to spend more on domestically made goods and services.

6. **Show your support.** Visit our website at www.free2Earn4Ever.com and buy a bumper sticker (but stick it on your vehicle window so you can remove it easily with a razor blade without damaging your vehicle). Purchase buttons, flyers, and other materials to show your support for the idea and to remind people that this idea is the answer for economic recovery, economic birth, personal freedom, and reclaiming ownership of our time.

7. **Get creative.** Do you already post videos online? Make up skits about what the world would be like if this plan was already a reality. How would people act? Would there be more people with video cameras? What would be an uploader's reaction if he or she checked his or her video account and saw a video had just gone viral and they had over one million hits in one week? It would be almost like winning the lottery.

8. **Use the templates.** The Free 2 Earn 4 Ever website offers many templates to print and hand out like a good little economic evangelist. Think about the hope you could bring someone by telling them about the possibility of earning money. Do you know anyone who could use a vacation but doesn't have the funds? Use one of our templates to print a list of video ideas he or she could create to sell. You would be giving them hope and making them aware of the talents and skills you see in them.

9. **Call your favorite radio stations or local news stations** and tell them you want them to know and talk about Free 2 Earn 4 Ever. It is a new opportunity that could change our world, and they need to be talking about it. Tell them to can it with all the entertainment news and talk about something that matters.

10. **Go to your favorite stores** and tell the managers they should carry the Free 2 Earn 4 Ever book in their stores. Everyone deserves the chance to read about the possibil-

ities before us. This is the book that will pivot us towards prosperity, and you want them to be part of it. If it is not a large chain store, you may even be able to think of online videos they could sell. If it is a store that sells food, perhaps they could produce a weekly cooking video. Try to think of videos the store could create that you would pay to watch. Businesses will benefit from the ability to sell online videos just as much as individuals. The whole idea of the Free 2 Earn 4 Ever campaign is that it levels the playing field and gives *anyone* the ability to earn.

11. **Throw your weight around.** This maxim brings about such fun mental pictures. If you own a business or work for a business, start talking about how your company would use this technology to boost your bottom line. On your website, find a space to show you support the Free 2 Earn 4 Ever idea. When businesses support the idea of earning equality, it shows they are not greedy and that they really care about fairness and the economic struggles impacting much of the world.

12. **Don't give up until this is in place.** You deserve to earn a living from your talents, knowledge, and stories. People get excited about ideas, but then they get busy doing other things, or another news story comes by and helps you forget about other stories. Don't let this be an idea that just fizzles out. This idea provides opportunity for people to change their lives and the way we live as a society. There is too much potential in this idea to let it be forgotten about.

The action items above are not intended to promote the sale of this book, which would be nice, but are instead intended to promote the idea behind this book. The idea behind the Free 2 Earn 4 Ever program is that there are endless possibilities for every person, every business, and every industry to create new revenue streams and to shape our world by selling value to viewers who want to be entertained, educated, and intrigued.

If you have enjoyed this book, or if it has gotten you thinking, ignited a little hope, and awoken some forgotten dreams, please rate this book and leave a comment about it on Amazon. com. Rating stars sell books. If you've never posted a comment about a book on Amazon, here are some pretty painless instructions: Log on to Amazon.com, click on the "Your Account" button, scroll down to the personalization section, and click "Your Public Profile." This will show you what information will show up next to your rating and comment. Once you like what you see here, go find the Free 2 Earn 4 Ever book (use the search box), then click the "Create your own review" link in the Customer Reviews section.

Thanks, and may God bless you!

CHAPTER 9

Frequently Asked Questions

Thus idea seems too good to be possible. If it was such a good idea, wouldn't we already have the ability to do this?

I thought the same thing, so I Googled it. After searching quite some time, I came across a video of a company explaining how large movie companies can provide their movies to a separate website where customers could rent the movies digitally. The video demonstrated how each company could select the price they wanted to charge for a consumer to watch the video and set different lengths of rental periods for different movies.

My first thought was, Yes! This is it! This technology is available! But wait. Why are they only giving this opportunity to big movie companies? It is the average person's videos that have made online videos what they are today. Why are they leaving the little guy out of the opportunity to make money?

In the few moments after realizing not only that this possible, but also that it was being pitched to big companies to make even more money, I became angry. My anger quickly subsided, and I decided to give this company the benefit of the doubt, telling myself that they just don't realize that offering this to everyone could have major benefits beyond the benefits currently offered to only the big companies.

However, it made me realize that I did not want to take this idea to Google, YouTube, or the companies offering this technology. Instead, I would take my idea to the people who upload millions of videos and the people who are frantically searching for jobs and ways to earn money.

Today, when a video is uploaded to YouTube, it has to get a minimum number of views before the uploader can add advertising to it. Once advertising is added, the uploader can earn a few cents every time a viewer clicks on an ad that displays over the top of the video. YouTube can also show a commercial before the video starts, and there is advertising revenue sharing for that, as well.

So to answer the question, at some point all the components come together, and it presents a window of opportunity to jump through and make things happen. Everything starts at some point. This starts now.

Is it healthy for people to get all their entertainment, news, and learning by sitting in front of their computers?

Nope! Some televisions and entertainment systems now allow a person to sit in their living room and watch videos from the Internet. Some televisions even come with a keyboard or keyboard remote so you can watch video playlists. You could create a lineup of the stories you wanted to watch for news. You will be able to watch videos just as easily as you watch television programming today.

In the details of your idea, the uploader has to pay an upload fee. Why doesn't the theme assembler have to pay a fee?

The upload fee is for the way the host company is compensated for storing a video on its servers. There may also be review requests by viewers who flag the video as being improperly titled, described, or rated, and the host company will not be reimbursed for its time investigating such issues. If a video is taken down for legal reasons, the uploader won't receive a refund of the upload fee. Charging an upload fee should prevent people from uploading junk. There will still be junk, but it's their money.

Would video stores contain videos uploaded by the theme assemblers who own the stores?
I don't know. There are a lot of details that need to be worked out. I would hope that people can find the best answers in a global conversation about this. The host companies that step forward to provide the platform for online video sales will need to actually build it. I am sure there are many more features that will make it great for everyone to use.

Why have a theme assembler role?
If a video receives a certain number of views on YouTube today, the uploader can start showing ads at the bottom of the video, which means the video earns money for the uploader. There are some people who copy popular videos and post them as their own so they can earn advertising revenue.

Having a theme assembler role will create more opportunities for people to earn money legally. In addition, assembling similar videos together adds value to viewers. There are many people who upload videos on a wide variety of subjects that will not appeal to everyone. It would be nice to be able to find videos that are similar in content or style, just like a store assembles products for specific groups of people. For example, clothing stores often pull together clothes and accessories of a certain style that appeals to a specific group of people. The same would be beneficial and convenient to viewers and would offer theme assemblers the opportunity for compensation. No one should be forced to work for free.

Anyone should be able to be a theme assembler. If you are interested in a particular subject, you can find videos that are helpful to you and assemble them for others interested in the same subject. You can add a fee layer on top of the video's original price to compensate you for your effort. Uploaders will be thankful you added their videos to your collection, because the videos are more likely to get purchased by being offered in your collection.

Why didn't you just start your own company to do this?

This is bigger than me. It is bigger than one company. The technical functionality components of this idea are owned by different companies. There will need to be a meeting of the minds to work together to create this. There is no way I could do this. I am just the idea person.

If someone has an idea but cannot carry it out, should he or she die with the idea? Should he or she not share the idea? Isn't it the right thing to do to share the idea so that someone else can carry it out?

Why didn't you go directly to some of these technology players to convince them to buy in?

People approach large companies all the time with ideas. I wanted people to be involved in the conversations with the technology players. The people who will be impacted by this deserve to know about it and push the technology companies to create this so that people can start earning a living sooner rather than when the companies get around to it someday. Large companies, for the most part, move cautiously with new ideas. They may wonder how much people would want it. They look out for their own interests first—their relationships with their advertisers and other businesses, for example. This idea needs to be out in the open so everyone is on the same page, moving forward to establish this online environment.

Why would people pay for videos when they can find the information for free on the Internet?

Why do people go to bookstores when they can borrow books from a library at no charge? Why do people pay for bottled water when they can drink from a faucet? For convenience and perceived value. It's their money; let them buy what they want.

Keep in mind it is not my goal to abolish free videos. I simply believe that people should have the freedom to charge a fee for their videos if they choose to do so. The value of the video should be determined by the person uploading it; it is then up to the viewer to agree and purchase or disagree and not purchase.

Can viewers use credits instead of money, like on Facebook?

People need to earn money, not credits or some other made-up currency. What if your employer asked you tomorrow to start working for tokens? Can you imagine paying the mortgage or rent with tokens? We need to cut out all the complicated junk.

People need and want money for their efforts. It is our common currency.

What if people post videos with information that isn't correct?
Can the same happen with products or books? Can a product not work? Can a book have information in it that is not right? If we don't move forward with this idea because some people might post a video with incorrect or inaccurate information, then we need to stop selling books, stop printing newspapers, stop manufacturing products, and shut down stores. Subpar videos will exist, but it doesn't diminish the positive impact this idea will have. It is worth the risk.

If store owners opted not to open a store because someone might steal from their store or a product they sell might be recalled, we would have no stores. This is no different. There are negative aspects to everything. If we focused only on what could go wrong in everything we do, we wouldn't do anything. Instead, we need to put safeguards in place to reduce negatives.

For example, if someone posts a video that claims wrinkles can be prevent by putting candy up your nose, I say let them post the video. Buyer beware, just like the way things are now. There are plenty of wrinkle creams that do not work, but it is up to the customer to decide whether or not to buy the product based on other customers' comments or reviews and common sense.

What if people buy a video and they don't like it?
There will be no refunds. They make things too complicated. Use common sense when making decisions about money. Pay attention viewer ratings and comments. This is already happening today with common products we purchase.

How can you prevent "bad people" from making money through videos and doing terrible things with it?
Do you know who you give your money to today when you purchase a product? Do you know how they money will be spent? Are you okay with it? Are the companies you buy products from

funding political parties you don't agree with? Are they spending their revenues on products that you wouldn't buy? The same concept will apply for online videos. If anything, this system will provide more transparency by looking at other types of videos an uploader is selling.

When will this online environment be available?
Good question. I don't know. I feel that my part is to share the idea and get people talking about it and understanding it. It is up to the readers to keep the conversation going and growing. The technology companies need to then respond to the conversations and demands for this technology environment. It will take a collective effort to create this video revolution that will indeed be a shift in globalization and an increase in prosperity. I can only imagine the positive impacts to the suffering economy we are all currently experiencing. Don't sit around waiting for this to happen. Read the chapter entitled "Make it Happen" and make it happen. This is an inevitable online environment. Be a part of creating it.

What if someone video tapes a movie or television show and uploads it to make money on it?
This is called piracy, and it is illegal. There will need to be upload guidelines that clearly help uploaders understand what is allowed and what isn't. There could even be guideline wizards to walk uploaders through a series of questions to help them determine if their videos will be approved. For example, the website could ask if a video contains images of a television show, movie, or other paid media. If the answer is yes, the uploader will be informed that the video is illegal. Guidelines will help. As with anything new, skills and rules must be taught.

This really seems like a win win-win situation. Who is the loser?
The loser is the person or company that doesn't want change. When I come up with ideas, I try to make them into win-win situations with no losers. However, employers currently

have a lot of influence and power because they are people's source of money, and this idea may scare them because people will be able to earn their own money without being completely dependent upon someone else for their livelihood.

FREE 2 EARN 4 EVER
WORKBOOK

People with potential

List five people you know that have interesting hobbies, stories, collections, talents, or a recent project that would make a great video.

1. Name:

What could he or she take a video of and sell?

How much would people pay to watch the video?

What could this person use the video earnings for? *(vacation, car, etc)*

2. Name:

What could he or she take a video of and sell?

How much would people pay to watch the video?

What could this person use the video earnings for? *(vacation, car, etc)*

3. Name:

What could he or she take a video of and sell?

How much would people pay to watch the video?

What could this person use the video earnings for? *(vacation, car, etc)*

4. Name:

What could he or she take a video of and sell?

How much would people pay to watch the video?

What could this person use the video earnings for? *(vacation, car, etc)*

5. Name:

What could he or she take a video of and sell?

How much would people pay to watch the video?

What could this person use the video earnings for? *(vacation, car, etc)*

NOTES:

Video Earning Potential

Grab a calculator and have fun with some video scenarios to understand the full potential of video earnings.

Video title:_____

Description:

a) Price per view:_____

b) Estimated monthly views:_____

c) Monthly revenue: (a*b = c)_____

d) Year one revenue: (c*12 = d)_____

e) In year two, five Theme Assemblers start selling this video and your views increase 20 times. How much did you earn in year two? (b*20*a*12= e)_____

For more scenarios, use the online calculator at
www.Free2Earn4Ever.com.

Money Is Made to be Spent

Think about how you would spend your video earnings. This is a good exercise and you may even discover things about yourself you were not aware of.

If you earned $200 per month on your videos, what would you spend that money on?

$1,000 per month?

$5,000 per month?

$10,000 per month?

Free 2 Earn 4Ever

If you had time to do anything you wanted, what would you do?

Where would you live if proximity to a job was not a factor?

150 years from now, your online videos are still earning loads of cash, who is receiving those funds? What charities or trusts would you want to funds to go to when you are no longer here?

What videos could you create and sell online?
Think about your passions, hobbies, and collections.

Who would you help get videos online to sell?
What organizations or individuals would you help?

NOTES:

One Million Dollars...

In the movie *Austin Powers*, one million dollars was considered to be a lot of money, but these days, many would say it is not much at all. Imagine that you uploaded a video and are selling it online. For the first few months, you are earning only a few dollars per month. One day, you check your account and your video has gone viral and there waiting for you is $1,000,000. How would you spend it? If you are thinking you will save it, what are you saving for? Will you eventually spend it?

Be specific in your description below. If you say you want to buy land, describe how much land and where. If you want to buy a car, what color, make and model is the car?

About the Author

From the age of five, S. J. August focused on earning money by inventing and selling things. A serial entrepreneur, she earned business and marketing degrees, and went on to travel around the United States selling magazines door-to-door. Ten hours a day, six days a week, were spent learning about people, their interests, and why they went to school and how they earned a living. For over ten years, August worked for a Fortune 500 company, where she helped create web applications that solved problems and streamlined business processes. Her recent book is entitled Free 2 Earn 4 Ever.